Virtual Field Trips

Virtual Field Trips

Gail Cooper
and
Garry Cooper

1997
Libraries Unlimited, Inc.
and Its Division
Teacher Ideas Press
Englewood, Colorado

LIBRARIES UNLIMITED, INC.
and Its Division
Teacher Ideas Press
P.O. Box 6633
Englewood, CO 80155-6633
1-800-237-6124
www.lu.com

Production Editor: Stephen Haenel
Copy Editor: Susan Brown
Proofreader: Susie Sigman
Layout and Design: Michael Florman

Library of Congress Cataloging-in-Publication Data

Cooper, Gail, 1950-
Virtual field trips / Gail Cooper and Garry Cooper.
xvii, 168 p. 19x26 cm.
Includes index.
ISBN 1-56308-557-7
1. Internet (Computer network) in education--United States.
2. World Wide Web (Information retrieval system). 3. School field trips--United States. I. Cooper, Garry. II. Title.
LB1044.87.C67 1997
025.06'37--dc21 97-26028
CIP

Dedication

To Jim and Jeff Markunas, to Alexandra Naomi Cooper, who learns from everything, and to School District 15 and the teachers at Winston Park Junior High, who encourage learning beyond the boundaries of the classroom.

Contents

INTRODUCTION

Imagine taking your students on a field trip without worrying about procuring transportation, finding chaperones, collecting fees and permission slips, and worrying about weather and lost and wandering children. Now, imagine such a trip completely unconstrained by the boundaries of place and time. That's how we've conceived *Virtual Field Trips,* and even teachers new to the Net will find getting on the virtual bus easier than the old-fashioned trips. Our goal in writing *Virtual Field Trips* is not only to let you know about the myriad of new learning experiences that are waiting for you and your students, but also to make it easy for you to get there. We've gone on each of these trips ourselves and checked thoroughly for appropriateness. And wait till you see what we've found!

Thanks to the Internet, you can expand your students' learning beyond the confines of the classroom walls. Museums, laboratories, libraries, schools, and modern and ancient cities around the world have opened their virtual doors and are waiting for your class to arrive. You can take your students to foreign countries, to the bottom of the ocean floor, and to the farthest reaches of outer space. You can spend an entire day with Thomas Jefferson at Monticello, visit da Vinci's workshop, view the Seven Wonders of the Ancient World, visit with famous authors, spend a winter at Valley Forge, tour the castles of Europe and Asia, plunder with the Vikings, swim with sharks, and participate in the Civil War. Your students can see museums around the world—both famous and obscure. The world's top laboratories, such as Los Alamos and Fermilab, have their virtual doors open, waiting for you. Take your students to powwow dances, travel through the human body, listen to the voices of Native Americans, whales, frogs, authors, and presidents (not necessarily in that order), visit other schools and classrooms, and view breathtaking photos from the Hubble telescope. Discover the Halls of Fame for women, African Americans, musicians, and pilots (male and female). Relive history's greatest triumphs and disasters.

Unlike movies and books, the Internet is interactive. Your students can ask scientists, astronauts, and mathematicians questions, watch frog dissections, participate in real-time discussions with students and professionals around the world, and exchange messages, music, writing, and art work with other classes. Best of all, many of the sites are regularly updated so you can visit over and over and keep up on the latest developments.

HOW TO USE THIS BOOK

Think of *Virtual Field Trips* as a carefully annotated guide book, arranged in a *Yellow Pages* format. Turn to the chapter of interest, where information will be arranged alphabetically by topic. Because so many of the places you'll visit cover a variety of disciplines, our categories are of necessity broad, so we urge you to check the index as well as the table of contents. In addition, we've extensively cross-referenced the listings. In testing *Virtual Field Trips* with educators, we've found that the net we've cast is extraordinarily wide, so we're sure you'll be able to find something that keys into your needs.

Remember that the Internet is extremely dynamic, and sites often change. This is one of its great advantages over textbooks and audio-visual aids—information is usually up-to-date. However, this also means that our descriptions of each field trip may not exactly match what you'll find when you visit the site.

We have assumed you already have access to the Internet and are familiar with the basics of Web browsing software, such as Netscape, Mosaic, or Internet Explorer. Several of the field trip sites have sound recordings, video clips, and QuickTime movies. Additional software is required to get the most from these sites. This software is often available at the site and can be downloaded to your computer for no charge other than your access time. Be warned, though, that downloading time can vary and may interrupt your field trip.

A word about museums and art galleries: You will find dozens of museums and art galleries listed in *Virtual Field Trips*. We have described many of the exhibits, but keep in mind that, just as with physical museums and galleries, on-line exhibits often change. We suggest you use our exhibit descriptions as general guides. If you're looking for material on the geological history of the Midwestern United States, for example, and our description of the Illinois State Museum talks about a Native American exhibit, you may still wish to check the site to see if a geological exhibit has been added. You can save time by bookmarking museums and galleries on your Web browser and checking your favorite sites every few months.

COMMON PROBLEMS

Occasionally you may find yourself confronted with a message that says, in effect, that the site is closed. This may occur for several reasons, none of which are your fault (unless you've typed an address incorrectly—be sure to type our addresses **exactly** as they appear in the book). The site may be temporarily closed for maintenance or updating, it may have moved, or, in rare instances, it may no longer accept visitors. Before you go home disappointed, try this: retype the address, eliminating segments of the address one by one, from right to left (going backwards toward the beginning). For example, if you can't connect to http://astro.uchicago.edu/cara/vtour, eliminate the vtour. If you still can't connect, eliminate cara. If you manage to connect this way, you may end up in a portion of the site different than what is described in *Virtual Field Trips*. It's like sneaking into a museum through a service entrance. Once you're in, start experimenting with different paths, and if you don't find your way to exactly what you're searching for, you will likely find a serendipitous surprise that also fits your needs. It's legal. Remember that the Internet is dynamic—that's both its strength and frustration; sites are often added, deleted, or rearranged. We hope you'll let us know when this occurs. (See *"Let Us Know!"* below.)

A WORD ABOUT SAFETY

By now you've heard about the commercials and inappropriate materials on the Internet. You'll be glad to know that we've carefully screened our field trips. If you use the same precautions as you would on an actual field trip—in other words, don't let your students wander around unattended—you don't have to worry.

LET US KNOW!

Just as many of the virtual field trips are interactive, this book can be seen as an interactive experience as well. Prior to publication, all of our field trips were checked for accuracy. However, as you wander around the world, you may find changes, additions, and deletions, as well as exciting new places. We encourage you to contact us with any ideas, requests, problems, or new field trips you've discovered. You can e-mail us at either: **gailc1@ix.netcom.com** or **gcoop@ix.netcom.com**. We're looking forward to hearing from you.

CHAPTER 1

Historic Time Travel

Instead of merely reading about people and events, why not *experience* them? Take your students directly to Civil War battles, spend time with such notables as Thomas Jefferson, and view the Seven Wonders of the Ancient World.

For sites of similar interest, see also Chapters 7, 8, and 12.

AFRICAN AMERICAN HISTORY

See also Chapter 8—National Civil Rights Museum; Chapter 10—Duke University Special Collections Library; *and* Chapter 12—King, Martin Luther Jr. *and* Malcolm X.

Duke University Special Collections Library

http://odyssey.lib.duke.edu/slavery

The *Third Person, First Person: Slave Voices* exhibit at this Duke University site examines the life and experiences of American slaves from the late eighteenth through the nineteenth century with details that bring the slavery experience into sharp focus. For example, there are invoices and shipping orders for slaves, writings by slaves, and letters about slaves from plantation owners.

Library of Congress—African-American Mosaic

http://lcweb.loc.gov/exhibits/african/intro.html

Experience life in the eighteenth and nineteenth century eras from slavery through the W.P.A. Roosevelt years. The exhibit is divided into four sections: Colonization, Abolition, Migration, and the W.P.A. The images and accompanying texts not only include maps and photographs, but original documents, such as a lifetime membership in the African Colonization Society. Precise exhibits of this kind convey the reality of the African American experience in a way that typical textbooks cannot.

Library of Congress—American Memory

http://lcweb.loc.gov/homepage/lchp.html

Take your students to the Library of Congress and follow the path **American Memory Home Page / Documents / African American Perspectives: Pamphlets from the Daniel A. P. Murray Collection / The Progress of a People**. They can then follow the struggle for and meet people instrumental in the quest for equality from Reconstruction through World War I. Attend the 1898 National African American Congress held in Washington, D.C., to "consider the status of the race." Free tickets are available for one or more of the following events: *Segregation and Violence*, *Solving the Race Problem*, and *Contributions to the Nation*. Notables, such as Bishop B. W. Arnett, John Brown, Frederick Douglass, Sergeant Major Christian Fleetwood, Kelly Miller, Mary Church Terrell, Ida B. Wells, and Booker T. Washington, address such topics as the repeal of the Black Laws of Ohio, mob violence and anarchy, the status of the "Lynch Law" in Georgia, and the church as a factor in solving the race problem. Both visual and audio materials are available.

National Civil Rights Museum

See Chapter 8—National Civil Rights Museum.

Negro Baseball League

http://www.blackbaseball.com

The *Negro Baseball League* was formally organized in 1920. This site, overseen by J. S. Riley, Director of Research for the Negro Leagues Baseball Museum in Kansas City, Missouri, examines the historical context of the formation of the league and chronicles its years in often eloquent language. Through texts and photographs, your students will be able to meet such players as Cool Papa Bell, known as the fastest man ever to play baseball. Cool Papa was officially clocked circling all of the bases in 12 seconds and was the only player ever to hit a triple on a bunt.

Negro Leagues Baseball Online Archive

http://www.infi.net/~moxie/nlb/nlb.html

This award-winning site covers the era of baseball from 1880-1955. Experience the realities of segregation as you read the historical *Black Ball News*, a journal that was devoted exclusively to the African American leagues. The league was so popular that an estimated 40,000 spectators attended the series playoffs in Chicago's Comiskey Park. Your students can also see photographs of and meet team members, such as Roy Campanella and Willie Mays, while learning about sports as well as life in the segregated United States. The impact of segregation comes alive with such stories as the team that waited on tables at a Florida resort at night and played baseball during the day. There is also a section about the Kansas City Monarchs, the team that featured Jackie Robinson, Ernie Banks, and Satchel Paige. You may want to avoid the gift shop, which sells posters and other memorabilia.

ALCATRAZ ISLAND

See Chapter 2—United States—California—Alcatraz Island.

AMERICAN REVOLUTION

See also Chapter 8—Library of Congress.

Valley Forge

http://www.libertynet.org/iha/valleyforge

For six months, Washington and his 12,000 soldiers—some of them as young as 12 years old—camped at Valley Forge, struggling against a harsh winter, low morale, and dwindling provisions. Now, thanks to the Valley Forge Historical Society, your class can visit the encampment and see weapons, uniforms, and other equipment, read the soldiers' actual journals and letters, and even view their personal effects. There is also a collection of Washington's personal effects. Some of the most famous people in American history will also be there. Find out why the Allen brothers may have been partially responsible for Benedict Arnold becoming a traitor. Your students will be able to join the boys and men of the Revolutionary War while they build huts for shelter, play cricket, and put on plays. They will also be able to meet the physicians and surgeons in field hospitals who worked for daily wages of $4.00 to $6.00 and participate in secret negotiations between Lafayette and Ben Franklin. You may want to read the on-site weather reports from 1775 before you embark on your journey.

Williamsburg, Virginia

http://www.history.org

The Colonial Williamsburg Foundation will take you on a tour of the area where the Revolutionary War was won. Some of the famous people you will meet include George and Martha Washington, Patrick Henry, and George Wythe—the gentleman who taught law to Jefferson and James Madison. Students will obtain a real feel for what colonial life was like by spending time with the Geddys, a family of tradesmen. The Geddys will take you through their home and through their foundry, where they craft guns, buckles, cutlery, and swords. You may prefer to spend time with the Randolphs, an influential family. Mr. Randolph presided over Virginia assemblies and chaired the first meeting of delegates from 13 colonies in Philadelphia in 1774. Feel free to wander through Gloucester Street to the Raleigh Tavern, where you are likely to run into Washington or Jefferson.

See also Chapter 12—Washington, George.

BOSNIAN CONFLICT

See Chapter 2—Bosnia—Civilian Tour.

CAMP DAVID ACCORDS

See Chapter 12—Carter, Jimmy, and Rosalynn Carter.

CIVIL RIGHTS

See African American History *above*.

CIVIL WAR

See also Chapter 8—The Lincoln Museum *and* Chapter 10—Duke University Special Collections Library.

Battle of Chickamauga

http://www.ptc.dcs.edu/cw/chick/index.html

Go back in time to September 19 and 20, 1863, and relive the Battle of Chickamauga from the perspectives of infantrymen. Students will be able to join former farmers, shopkeepers, and other citizens as they battle for Chattanooga, a key rail center and gateway to Confederate territory. Texts are accompanied by photographs of the land, so you can get a good sense of how topography influenced strategies and outcomes. Also included is a bibliography and a history of the 19th Alabama Infantry.

Battle of Gettysburg

http://www.gettysburg.com

The Civil War was the first war to be photographed, and this collection of photographs and textual material helps you feel like you're actually revisiting the Battle of Gettysburg. You will be able to meet and see the people involved in the battle (General John Buford and his aides, General James Longstreet, General George Meade, and Union officers), and see and read about Cemetery Hill; Civil War equipment, such as spurs, saddles, and Custer's nonregulation uniform (which he specially designed so his troops would easily find him in battle); the battle itself (calvary men battling with soldiers at Brandy Station, an exploding shell at Cemetery Hill, Meade conducting a war council, etc.); and Pickett's famous charge. The materials are divided into *People*, *Equipment*, *Battles*, *Panorama*, and *The Horrors of War*.

Battle of Mobile Bay

http://www.maf.mobile.al.us/recreation/area_history/battle.html

This exhibit is a tribute to the Battle of Mobile Bay—known not only as the naval battle that was the "beginning of the end for the Confederacy" but also as the first battle in which all new technological developments of modern warfare were present, including iron ships, rifled guns, explosive shells, and mines. Your students will start their trip in the early morning hours of August 5, 1864, as the federal fleet begins its attack on Fort Morgan. Watch as wooden ships are lashed together in pairs and led by the Tecumseh and other ironclad ships. Although the Tecumseh will be lost when it hits a mine, the battle will be the first major success of General Ulysses S. Grant's strategy to re-elect Lincoln in 1864 and end the Civil War by military victory rather than negotiated peace.

Battle of Olustee

http://extlab1.entnem.ufl.edu/olustee

The Battle of Olustee was the largest Civil War battle in the state of Florida. This site is primarily text-based, and its most vivid parts (aside from the impressive facts and analyses) are primary-source documents, such as actual letters written from the battlefront. Also included are photographs of Winston and Octavius Stephens (Lt. of the 2nd Florida Cavalry and his wife) and Civil War uniforms and accoutrements, such as shirts and vests, trousers and suspenders, overcoats and ponchos, hats, kepis, buttons, belts and buckles, and supplies.

Civil War Center

http://www.cwc.lsu.edu

The United States Civil War Center, at Louisiana State University, has more than 18,000 public and private documents and photos, including such things as the governments' standing orders for the Union Army, the official Massachusetts casualty list, lists of Jewish American soldiers, individual states' emancipation proclamations, Jefferson Davis's personal papers, and pictures and texts on Confederate symbols.

Civil War Women

http://odyssey.lib.duke.edu/collections/civil-war-women.html

The *Civil War Women* exhibit contains scanned images and transcripts of writings of women from the Civil War era. Meet such women as Rose O'Neal Greenhow—one of the most renowned spies of the Civil War. She was so successful at her occupation that Jefferson Davis credited the victorious Battle of Manassas to her efforts. You may also want to meet the more innocent 16-year-old Alice Williamson. Her diary chronicles the occupation of Gallatin and the surrounding region by Union forces.

Diaries

http://jefferson.village.virginia.edu/vshadow2

The University of Virginia has come up with this excellent idea for understanding the Civil War as part of a series of projects designed to incorporate new communications technology into education. Extensive data from two towns in Virginia and Pennsylvania (towns that despite being only about 100 miles apart are on opposite sides of the Mason-Dixon Line) have been archived. Students can see photographs, maps, letters, diaries, county records, and newspaper articles covering Civil War era lives and culture in vivid and minute detail. The material covers the period of time from the late 1850s (during the time of John Brown's raid) to April of 1861, the start of the Civil War. Site administrators suggest that teachers and classes use the raw data to construct their own narratives. Several examples, such as the role of women in the Civil War, of Free Blacks on both sides of the Mason-Dixon Line, and of Irish-born residents, are included on site.

Galutia York

http://www.snymor.edu/pages/library/local_history/civil_war

Galutia York was a 19 year old from Hubbardsville, New York, who responded to President Lincoln's request for volunteers to fight in the Civil War. Less than one year later, after seeing several battles, he died of an illness. Colgate University has collected letters written by York, as well as maps and photographs, including the hospital at Fort Monroe, Virginia, where he died.

Library of Congress Photographs

http://rs6.loc.gov/cwphome.html

This Library of Congress site contains over 1,100 Civil War photographs, most of which were taken under the supervision of Matthew Brady. Photographic subjects include military personnel and scenes of battle preparations and "after-effects." You can search for a particular photograph by keyword or by subject matter. Also included is a Civil War timeline and a bibliography.

Music and Poetry

http://www.erols.com/kfraser

General Robert E. Lee contended that "there would have been no army without music." This site contains song lyrics and poetry written by soldiers rather than professional or polished poets. In addition to being divided into Confederate and Union poems, the exhibit is further divided into subsections, such as *Battles*, *Officers*, *A Soldier's Life*, and *Post-War Reminiscences*.

http://www2.tsixroads.com/Corinth_MLSANDY/songsciv.html

Songs were an integral part of the Civil War. The *Civil War Songbook* contained in this exhibit has the lyrics to dozens of well-known and obscure songs, including *The Battle Cry of Freedom* (George Root, 1862), *Marching Through Georgia* (Henry Clay Work, 1865), *All Quiet Along the Potomac Tonight*, *Hard Tack*, and *The Army Bean*.

Southern Historical Collection—University of North Carolina

http://ils.unc.edu/civilwar/civilwar.html

If you believe that learning about the *experience* of war is as important as learning the facts, you and your students will want to visit the Southern Historical Collection at the University of North Carolina. Letters written by Confederate and Union soldiers directly from the battlefront describe the wounding of Stonewall Jackson, the Battle of Gettysburg, day-to-day soldiering, and separation from loved ones. Students can select the letters they wish to read by clicking on a map, a soldier's name, or a battle.

EGYPT, ANCIENT

See also Chapter 2—Egypt; Chapter 6—World Art Treasures; *and* Chapter 8—Duke Papyrus Archive, Egyptology, Emory University Museum's Ancient Egypt Gallery, Institute of Art and Archaeology, Kelsey Museum at the University of Michigan, *and* Oriental Institute—University of Chicago.

http://pharos.bu.edu/Egypt/Alexandria

Take your students on a tour of Alexandria, from its ancient beginnings to modern restaurants. See where Anthony and Cleopatra met. Graphics include historical plans, maps, drawings, and photos. Your students may also wish to wander into the "auditorium" and listen to a performance of local music.

For other information contained in this site, see Seven Wonders of the Ancient World, *below*.

ELLIS ISLAND

See Chapter 11—Schools—United States—Washington—Alderwood Elementary School—Bellingham.

GREECE, ANCIENT

See Chapter 2—Greece.

GULF WAR

http://www.pbs.org/wgbh/pages/frontline/gulf/index.html

Thanks to the PBS *Frontline* series, your students can watch the Gulf War all over again. There is a wealth of vivid material, including photographs and maps. Challenge your students' gender expectations by showing the interview with Major Rhonda Cornum, who was on a search and rescue mission when her helicopter was shot down. With broken arms and other injuries, she was captured by the Iraqis. Her story begins (you can read it or hear it) when the Iraqis discover that she is female. Other sections include weapons and technology, interviews with the political and military decision makers, analyses by two journalists, and an interview with the Iraqi Foreign Minister, Tariq Assiz.

HOLOCAUST

http://remember.org

The *Holocaust Cybrary*, an immense site, attempts to make the horrors of the Holocaust real and immediate through stories, experiences, and dynamic discussions. Administrator Mike Dunn is especially interested in promoting discussion with high school students. Unlike other Holocaust sites, the *Cybrary* avoids the more famous authors and focuses on poems, articles, and book excerpts from survivors and relatives of survivors. Each year in April, the *Cybrary* plans to hold a live, interactive discussion with Holocaust authorities and anyone else who wishes to participate. The previous year's discussion is preserved on site. There are sections containing parents' stories as related by their children and information on lost family tracing. The latter will alert students to the immediacy of the experience for so many people today and will increase their awareness of the research possibilities of the Internet. Also included are a complete curriculum and a teacher's guide.

HORSE, HISTORY OF

http://www.imh.org

Although the first horses were no larger than a fox, they and their descendants became an integral part of world history. The International Horse Museum presents an interesting historical tour organized by the various roles played by the horse. The tour begins in 56 B.C. and covers such notables and eras as Atilla the Hun, the early draft horse in America, and soldiers on the western frontier. There are also audio-visual files of the famous race between Man o' War and Sir Barton on October 12, 1920, and race calls from Kentucky Derbies (1941-1968).

MAYANS

Mayaquest

http://www.mecc.com/mayaquest.html or
gopher://informns.k12.mn.us
Path: Minnesota K12 Resources / Mayaquest

Embark on a tour of modern and ancient Mayan country. This tour is based on a January 1995 expedition, in which a team of cyclists embarked on a "wholly kid directed expedition" into Belize, Guatemala, Honduras, and Mexico to study the ancient Mayan world. Carrying laptop computers and utilizing satellites, the team was linked to schools and homes via the Internet to enable communication with children around the world. Although the expedition is over, resources and materials for interdisciplinary studies are still available on site. There are units on environmental perspectives, war, contemporary Mayan people, creation myths and other tales, archaeology, deciphering hieroglyphics, and animals of the rain forest. You might want to take your students on the Mayaquest scavenger hunt, where they gather clues and piece together their own hypotheses about what happened to the Mayan civilization. There are many more activities and numerous exhibits, including Mayan death masks, flags, and art.

Visit with the Mayans

http://www.halfmoon.org

Visit this site and learn how to make your own Mayan calendar or monument, how to write your name in Mayan hieroglyphics, and how to play Mayan games (compete with each other or a computer). You will also be able to hear Yucatec sounds and see palaces and pyramids. You can even learn how to be attractive to other Mayans should you meet any along the way—shape your head, arrange your eyes, and decorate your teeth.

MCCARTHY ERA

See Chapter 12—McCarthy, Joseph.

MEDIEVAL CASTLES

See Chapter 2—United Kingdom—Welsh Castles.

NATIVE AMERICAN HISTORY

See Chapter 8—Indians of the Americas.

OLYMPICS, ANCIENT

http://devlab.dartmouth.edu/olympic

Students can take a self-guided tour of the Ancient Olympic Games Virtual Museum. The tour begins in the museum lobby from which you can enter such rooms as the Hall of Definitions and the Anecdotes Room. There are interviews with Dartmouth professors who reveal how cheating was dealt with, what awards were given, and why the original games ended. Females will have to stay within the museum as the ancient Greek government strictly forbids women to watch the games. When the games are over you may want to tour ancient Greece and see the temples of Zeus and Hera and other landmarks.

OREGON TRAIL

See Chapter 11—Schools—United States—Wyoming.

PALEOLITHIC PAINTED CAVE

http://www.culture.fr/culture/gvpda-en.htm

A vast network of underground caves decorated with paintings and engravings dating from the Paleolithic Age has recently been discovered in the south of France. Students will be able to experience historical spelunking—not only exploring caves, but studying about ancient cultures. Your host is the Minister of Culture and the Biblioteque Universalis, so you're in good company. An added bonus is that this site is also presented in French.

PIRATES OF THE CARIBBEAN

http://orion.it.luc.edu/~tgibson/pirates/pirates.html

It's off to the Caribbean and back in time to learn all about pirates. In addition to a complete listing of pirates and their ships, your class can learn the difference between pirates, privateers, and freebooters. They will also be able to learn about and see pictures of some of the most famous pirates, such as Henry Morgan and Blackbeard, as well as female pirates, such as Mary Read and Anne Bonny. The section on pirate myths and facts is full of surprises. For instance, pirates really did pierce their ears—it was believed that gold and silver embedded in the ears would improve eyesight. Learn the awful truth about marooning—those convicted of crimes were left on barren sand pits rather than on lush islands where they had a chance of survival. Show your students various pistols and flags and read the codes by which pirates lived. The similarities and differences between the harsh democracy of pirate ships and other democratic societies will spur some interesting classroom discussions.

PLYMOUTH PLANTATION

http://media3.com/plymouth/vtour

Take your students on a tour of "Plimouth Plantation," the first permanent European settlement in southern New England. They can see photographs of a reconstructed 1627 Pilgrim village, Hobbamock's homesite, and the Nye barn, where attempts are being made to reproduce the exact way animals looked 350 years ago. There are also reproductions of clothing, boats, art work, and tools. Although there is little narrative at this site, the photographs are fascinating,

PREHISTORIC TIMES

See Chapter 8—American Museum of Natural History, Cambrian Explosion, College of Eastern Utah Prehistoric Museum, Field Museum of Natural History, Museum of Antiquities, Paleontology, Paleontology Without Walls, *and* Royal British Columbia Museum.

ROME, ANCIENT

See Chapter 6—Detroit Institute of the Arts.

SEVEN WONDERS OF THE ANCIENT WORLD

http://pharos.bu.edu/Egypt/Wonders

Only one of the seven wonders of the ancient world, the Great Pyramid of Giza, is in existence today. This virtual field trip, however, will allow your students to see all of the wonders, including the Lighthouse of Alexandria, the Colossus of Rhodes, the Mausoleum at Halicarnassus, the Temple of Artemis at Ephesus, the Statue of Zeus at Olympia, and the Hanging Gardens of Babylon. This award-winning site also features other ancient and modern manmade and natural wonders, such as Angkor Wat in Cambodia, Niagara Falls, the Eiffel Tower, and the Great Wall of China.

SOVIET UNION—SOVIET ARCHIVES

http://sunsite.unc.edu/expo/soviet.exhibit/soviet.archive.html

The materials at this Library of Congress site are the first public display of highly secret internal records of Soviet Communist rule. Eavesdrop on a discussion held with the Soviet archivist that explains how and why the materials were accumulated. You can then participate in the internal workings of the Soviet Union from 1917 to the present, read letters from Gorky to Stalin, learn about the secret police and collectivization, experience the problems of the intelligentsia and dissidents like Boris Pasternak, learn about the deportation of Tatars following World War II, read the internal investigation results of the nuclear incident at Chernobyl, and experience the implications of the Cold War.

TITANIC

http://www.fireflyproductions.com/titanic

Take your students on a virtual tour of the *Titanic*, from the boat deck to the boiler room. Meet the crew members and passengers and see photographs of the ill-fated ship, including the famous grand staircase. Information on the survivors (there are only nine left) and other current issues covered in this exhibit is updated frequently. The exhibit is filled with facts and trivia, as well as information about the lives of the survivors after the tragedy—details that make one realize the enormity of the tragedy.

UNITED KINGDOM—TOWER OF LONDON

See Chapter 2—United Kingdom.

VIKINGS

The Vikings Association

http://www.student.gu.se/~daha0002/elveeng.htm

An association of Swedish students wants to help the world learn about Viking culture. Presently the site is in Swedish and consists of photos of the students in authentic Viking clothes, wandering around the country, but they promise to expand the site and add English text. In the meantime, they furnish links to other Viking information, and the photos are a lot more interesting than Richard Widmark in his Hollywood Viking costume.

The World of Vikings

http://www.n-vision.com/spoon/vikes/index.html

This site was established to dispel common myths and misconceptions about the Vikings and Viking culture. For example, students will learn that Vikings never wore horned helmets or furry boots. The introduction to the site is rather flippant, but the material that follows on Viking ornamentation, footwear, and social strata is detailed and serious. The images of art, artifacts, clothing, and other aspects of Viking life are keyed directly to the texts. The author takes his Viking research so seriously that he has even adopted a Viking name.

A WALK THROUGH TIME

http://physics.nist.gov/GenInt/Time/time.html

Students can take a virtual tour through the evolution of time measurement, from ancient calendars through the earliest clocks to the "Atomic Age of Time Standards." They'll be in safe hands with the National Institute of Standards and Technology, an agency of the Technology Administration of the Department of Commerce.

WATERGATE

See Chapter 12—Nixon, Richard M.

WORLD WAR I

http://lcweb.loc.gov/homepage/lchp.html

The Library of Congress has an extensive collection of World War I documents, images, and audio recordings accessible via the path **American Memory Project / Sound Recordings / Recordings from World War I and the 1920 Election**. You can follow the events leading to the war and meet and hear such notables as General John Pershing, James Watson Gerard, and Samuel Gompers. There is also a multimedia exhibit covering the presidential election of 1920 (Warren G. Harding and Calvin Coolidge on the Republican ticket and James Cox and Franklin Delano Roosevelt on the Democratic ticket).

For other information contained in this site, see Chapter 8—Library of Congress.

WORLD WAR II

See also Chapter 8—National Archives and Records Administration.

A-Bomb Museum

See Chapter 8—A-Bomb Museum.

Female Journalists, Photographers, and Broadcasters of World War II

http://lcweb.loc.gov/exhibits/wcf/wcf0001.html

World War II marked the first major foray of women into the work force and offered one of the first professional opportunities for female journalists. This Library of Congress exhibit spotlights eight women who succeeded in going to the front during the war: Therese Bonney, Toni Frissell, Marvin Breckenridge Patterson, Clare Booth Luce, Janet Flanner, Esther Bubley, Dorothea Lange, and May Craig.

First-Person Accounts

http://www.islandnet.com/~awong/war/index.html

Andrew Wong is collecting stories from people all over the world whose grandfathers fought in World War II. His mission is to promote peace by uniting everyone through the stories of their relatives, and many of the stories are powerful in their simplicity. A Filipino girl writes of her grandfather who was walking down a road when the soldier directly behind him died from a bullet that hit him in the head. Her grandfather recalls thinking calmly that God had decided for some reason another soldier and not he should die that day. The story is even more poignant because her grandfather is dead, and her father told her the story—she had never even known her grandfather had fought in a war. Students can e-mail directly to the people who post their stories

National Archives and Records Administration Exhibit Hall

http://www.nara.gov/exhall/people/people.html

The United States federal government's National Archives and Records Administration exhibit, *People at War*, highlights the contributions of thousands of American military personnel and civilians who served during World War II. There is a detailed background on events leading up to the war. The tour covers both the Pacific and European theaters. You can learn about the Sullivan brothers, whose deaths led to the passage of the Sullivan Law, which exempted at least one son from serving, so that no family would ever again lose all its sons. You can also meet Doris Miller, an African American sailor who machine gunned down several Japanese planes from the deck of the USS *Virginia* during the attack on Pearl Harbor, yet still encountered institutionalized racism. Meet members of the special units formed to accommodate minorities, such as the *Code Talkers*, a unit of Navajo Indians used for radio transmissions. They tell us that the Japanese were never able to break their "coded" transmissions. You will also be able to meet famous military personnel and women who served in the war. Look in on the war in Europe and meet Joe Kennedy. You can examine the role scientists played in the development of the DUKW (the amphibious trucks that we call ducks) and the development of the M-1 Garand rifle. Stick around until the end and attend the meeting of American and Russian troops at the Elbe, meet the 509th composite group who flew the first A-bomb mission, and attend the surrender ceremony.

For other information contained at this site, see Chapter 8—National Archives and Records Administration.

Patch American High School Exhibit

http://192.253.114.31/D-Day/Table_of_Contents.html

The students of Patch American High School in Stuttgart, Germany, have put together an exhibit on World War II from material collected from government and military archives. Your students can obtain illustrated booklets on such topics as the Normandy Invasion, descriptions of D-Day invasion sites, the Army Nurse Corps, General Omar Bradley, and military campaigns. There is also an extensive photographic collection and various government documents, including speeches, maps, and battle plans.

CHAPTER 2

Worldwide Travel

Of course, around the world in 80 days seems merely quaint. How about around the world in 80 minutes? To avoid vaccinations, passports, language problems, and jet lag, take the following virtual field trips that literally cover the Earth from pole to pole. Now you can go to Antarctica at the same time you're complaining about the classroom air conditioning that's not working.

AFGHANISTAN

See Chapter 3—Natural Wonders—Himalayas.

AFRICA

See Chapter 6—African Art.

ALGERIA

See Arab Countries *below*.

AMAZON RAINFOREST

See Chapter 3—Natural Wonders—Rainforests.

ANTARCTICA

McMurdo Station

http://astro.uchicago.edu/cara/vtour

The Center for Astrophysical Research in Antarctica uses photographs taken from weather satellites to give you a bird's-eye view of the South Pole and the McMurdo Station. The texts, accompanied by on-the-ground photos, focus on the research facilities and equipment.

On-line Tour #1

http://icair.iac.org.nz/education/resource/homepage/homepage.htm

The International Center for Antarctica Information and Research, with the assistance of Pet Sommerville, a New Zealand education consultant, provides detailed information covering Antarctic weather, geological features, history, flora and fauna, science programs, treaties, and culture, as well as a glossary and a bibliography. Teachers may want to begin by reading the *Teacher Notes*, which provide an overview of and rationale for this site. Student self-study units cover biology, ecology, anatomy, experimental design, scientific interpretation, weather, and environmental issues. Sommerville is attempting to make this a more interactive site by requesting lesson plans from teachers around the world and by letting students read what other students have posted in the self-study units.

On-line Tour #2

http://quest.arc.nasa.gov/antarctica/index.html

Live From Antarctica is an electronic field trip to the Palmer Peninsula, a center for marine biology and ecological research. The trip is sponsored by the National Aeronautics and Space Administration (NASA). NASA schedules the trip during the time of year when students can see baby seals and penguins in their birth colonies and rookeries. In addition to local scenery and animal life, the trip provides information on global climate change, the stability of the Antarctic ice shelves and sheets and the ozone holes. Teachers can study the on-site classroom activities and teacher guides while students read scientists' field journals and view pictures. Questions can be directly e-mailed to NASA staff, and answers are posted on line.

South Pole Observatory

http://www.cmdl.noaa.gov/spo/spo.html

The South Pole Observatory maintains monitoring programs for greenhouse and other trace gases, atmospheric aerosols, solar radiation variability, stratospheric ozone, etc., and conducts field programs to understand chemical changes in the Antarctic region that might impact climate and global change. Students can obtain the latest temperature and atmospheric readings from the South Pole and other observation stations around the world. Current and back issues of the *New South Polar Times*, a newsletter written by staff members at the observation station, provide interesting and fun glimpses of life in the Antarctic. One entry, for example, describes the 300 Club. If you want to join, you must wait until the temperature drops to -100° F, take a +200° F nude sauna, run outside to the South Pole marker, and then run back inside before you freeze to death.

ARAB COUNTRIES

http://www.arab.net/welcome.html

This will take you to the home page of Arabnet, one of the most thorough Internet sources of information on Arab countries. Click on the flag of any country you wish to visit, and you will find detailed information on its history, geography, business, culture, government, transportation, and famous sites. Countries represented are Algeria, Bahrain, Egypt, Iraq, Jordan, Kuwait, Lebanon, Morocco, Oman, Qatar, Saudi Arabia, Sudan, Syria, Tunisia, the United Arab Emirates, and Yemen.

AUSTRALIA

See also Chapter 3—Botanic Gardens—Australian Botanic Gardens; Chapter 11—Schools—Australia; *and* Chapter 13—Australia.

http://australia-online.com

Learn all about Australia through texts, images, and sounds. The site includes typical facts one might glean from standard texts, as well as collections of photographs. You can even learn to speak Strine (fair dinkum Aussie) just like a true blue ocker.

BAHRAIN

See Arab Countries *above.*

BANGLADESH

http://www.asel.udel.edu/~kazi/bangladesh/bd_contents.html

Visit Bangladesh at this award-winning site. There are maps, facts, and information about Bangladesh history, geography, government and economy, literature, art and music, and people, culture, and lifestyles. You can even hear the national anthem and learn Bangla, the national language.

BHUTAN

See Chapter 3—Natural Wonders—Himalayas.

BOSNIA

Civilian Tour

http://geog.gmu.edu/gess/jwc/bosnia/bosnia.html

This virtual tour of Bosnia was organized by Jeremy Crampton and Beth Rundstrom of the Department of Geography at Virginia's George Mason University. The confusing Bosnian conflict comes into sharp focus through this step-by-step tour, which Crampton and Rundstrom begin by taking you back into history. Through concise texts and maps, which change scale to clarify the shifting events, your students can learn the origins of the Bosnian conflict. The tour continues through time to the Dayton Peace Accords, with each section of the tour containing questions that test and stretch student understanding. At the end of the tour, students are requested to choose a role, such as a refugee from Zepa or a United Nations' peacekeeper in Gorazde, and then answer questions from their chosen perspective. Finally, students and teachers are requested to e-mail their comments about the tour.

Military Tour

http://www.dtic.mil/bosnia/index.html

BosniaLINK is the official Department of Defense information system about United States and United Nations Bosnian military operations. There are maps, fact sheets, news releases, biographies, photographs, and transcripts of briefings, speeches, and testimony. You can also obtain the current copy of *The Talon*, the official newspaper for U.S. troops in Bosnia, or send an e-mail message directly to the troops.

BURMA

See Myanmar, *below*.

CAMBODIA

See Thailand, *below, and* Chapter 1—Seven Wonders of the Ancient World.

CANADA

See also Pacific Northwest Coast Indians, *below;* Chapter 8—Glenbow; *and* Chapter 9—Science—Museums—Aviation and Aerospace.

Lake Academy—Fortune, Newfoundland

http://www.k12.nf.ca/lakeacademy

The students of Lake Academy, a K-9 school located in Fortune, Newfoundland, want to show you their town. They will take you on a tour of their school as well as local sights, such as the town's ferry, trailer park, highway, and international fish processing plant. If you have time, stick around for the social studies class and learn all about Newfoundland and Labrador.

Leo Ussak School—Canadian Arctic

http://www.arctic.ca/LUS

The Leo Ussak elementary school claims to be the "coolest school in Canada's arctic." Students invite you to visit their school and meet the staff, read their school newsletter (in either English or Inuktitut), see maps, and learn about Leo Ussak (an elder of the Inuit), the Rankin Inlet, and the language of the Inuit. While you're there, be sure to visit the Students' Gallery, which contains northern tales, art, and student multimedia projects.

National Atlas of Canada

See Chapter 10—National Atlas of Canada.

Northumberland Strait Bridge

http://www.peinet.pe.ca/SCI/bridge.html

It is rare that one can view the actual construction of a major bridge as it occurs—particularly one that will be the longest continuous multispan marine bridge in the world. The Northumberland Strait Bridge, which connects Prince Edward Island with mainland New Brunswick and Nova Scotia, was just completed in 1997. This site allows students to view the bridge as it was being built, through actual photographs and drawings. The "island cam" shows a new live image of the area every 15 minutes. There are also detailed plans and archived photos of the construction for students who wish to delve deeper into engineering concepts.

CASTLES

See also United Kingdom—Welsh Castles, *below.*

http://fox.nstn.ca/~tmonk/castle/castle.html

Ted Monk, a castle enthusiast, will take you on a worldwide tour of literally dozens of European and Asian castles. Each tour includes photographs and detailed historical information. There is also a bibliography and a glossary of castle terms. Ian Burns, an eight year old, has posted his views on castles as well. In his section on castle defenses, Ian points out that defenders "used boiling water and sometimes they threw dead cows out of the castle to spread disease among the enemy (and as a stink bomb too)." If you're interested in buying a castle, check out the on-site real estate listings.

CENTRAL AMERICA

See also Guatemala, *below.*

Project Central America

http://www.adventureonline.com/pca

This is a two-month, 1,900-mile learning adventure designed by the Minnetonka, Minnesota, public school system and the Bush Educational Leadership Program. The site contains teaching materials, an electronic textbook, language tutors, maps, and photographs.

CHINA

See also Chapter 1—Seven Wonders of the Ancient World.

On-line Tour #1

http://pasture.ecn.purdue.edu/~agenhtml/agenmc/china/china.html

Students of Purdue University will take you on a tour of China where you will be able to view works of art and scenery. Guided tours include the Forbidden City, the Great Wall, and the Imperial Garden. Don't forget to sample the food while you're there with the illustrated Chinese Cookbook.

On-line Tour #2

http://www.chinapage.com

Learn all about classical Chinese art, calligraphy, poetry, history, literature, painting, and philosophy through texts and images. This site has more of a cultural focus than the first tour.

EGYPT

See also Arab Countries, *above;* Chapter 1—Egypt, Ancient; Chapter 6—Detroit Institute of the Arts *and* World Art Treasures; *and* Chapter 8—Egyptology.

On-line Tour

http://www.memst.edu/egypt/main.html

Most tourists who visit Egypt follow the same circuit—from Cairo, to Luxor, to Abu Simbel, with all points in between. This virtual tour follows the same route, with photographs and informative texts highlighting the most important and interesting facts.

For additional information on this site, see Chapter 8—Institute of Art and Archaeology.

ENGLAND

See United Kingdom, *below*.

FRANCE

See also Chapter 5—Theater—Phantom of the Opera.

Le Cordon Bleu Cooking School

http://sunsite.unc.edu/expo/restaurant/restaurant.html

Students can visit the world famous Le Cordon Bleu cooking school in Paris and meet Chef Andre L. Cointreau, the Cointreau family, and the Remy Martins, all of whom will be more than happy to share recipes and teach you the fundamentals and philosophy of French cuisine, advanced cooking techniques, and the history of Le Cordon Bleu, dating back to 1896. Although the recipes are for haute cuisine and require difficult and sophisticated cooking techniques, everything is clearly explained. Home economics teachers may enjoy altering (or savaging) these recipes.

Paris

http://sunsite.unc.edu/wm/paris

This site allows you to choose between touring Paris on your own or with a guide, and you also have a choice between touring in English or French. Either tour will allow you to see famous French sites, including the Catacombs, the Louvre, the Champs-Elysee, the Arc de Triomphe, the Eiffel Tower, Notre Dame Cathedral (*sans* hunchback), and other famous landmarks.

GERMANY

Bus Stops of Hannover

http://www.x-com.de/busstops/index.html

When you're on a virtual field trip, even the bus stops become an event, especially when you're in Hannover, Germany. As part of Hannover's "Art in the Public Sphere" project, nine designers were commissioned to create nine bus and tram stops for the city, all of which are presented on this tour. The intent of the designs was to change the passive empty experience of waiting for a bus into a sensory experience. Our favorite stop along the tour was Wolfgang Laubersheimer's creation, which features parabolic reflectors that allow you to hear what people at the bus stop across the street are saying.

On-line Tour #1: Berlin

http://www.chemie.fu-berlin.de/adressen/berlin.html

Tours of Berlin are available in English, German, or French. Students can take a guided tour or wander around the city on their own. A detailed on-site map will prevent them from getting lost while they see and learn about the Berlin Wall, Brandenburg Gate, and other buildings and landmarks.

On-line Tour #2: Nuremberg

http://www.wi2.uni-erlangen.de/NueTour/index.html

This is the starting point for guided tours of Nuremberg's castles, landmarks, and other sites. An on-site map is provided for the more adventuresome who prefer to explore on their own. Either way, there is a wealth of information about local history and culture, as well as links to other information on Bavaria.

On-line Tour #3

http://192.253.114.31/Travel_spots/travel_center.html

The students of Patch American High School will take you on a tour of Stuttgart, Augsburg, and Berlin during which you will be able to learn German history, participate in local holidays, and see the Mercedes-Benz and Porsche Museums. Of particular interest is the exhibit on the Berlin Wall, which was put together by Patch American students and 30 different worldwide schools. Your students will be able to either read or hear the history of the wall and the Berlin Airlift, personal stories of visits to the wall, speeches, the history of the Cold War, and German, American, and European perspectives on unification.

For other information contained in this site, see Chapter 11—Schools—Germany—Patch American High School—Stuttgart, Germany.

GHANA

http://www.uta.fi/~csfraw/ghana.html

Despite travel warnings by the United States Department of State, students can still visit Ghana courtesy of Francis Akoto, a native Ghanian and design engineer for Noki Telecommunications. Before beginning the journey, we suggest that students view the on-site materials with directions to Ghana and warnings and advice on travel within the country. Reading the available on-site information about the local currency and current events will enable them to make wise consumer decisions and give them things to discuss with the people they'll be meeting. Once in Ghana, they can view the local sites while learning about the climate and geography, people and culture, history, sports, and local cuisine. There is even a copy of Ghana's Top 10 Music Chart. Akoto has also assembled a large collection of links, including one to the Miss Ghana home page.

GREAT BRITAIN

See United Kingdom, *below*.

GREECE

See also Chapter 1—Olympics, Ancient *and* Seven Wonders of the Ancient World *and* Chapter 6—Detroit Institute of the Arts.

Hellenic Culture and Civilization

http://www.greekcivil.ariadne-t.gr/default.html

This extensive site covers almost every aspect of Hellenic civilization by providing access to the museums of Greece and Cyprus, the literature of such writers as Plato, and arts and music. The site is far too extensive to include a description of all available materials, but navigation is easy and self-explanatory through such categories as *Art Museums*, *Galleries of Art*, *Historical Museums*, *Maritime Museums*, *Museums of Natural History*, *Theatrical Museums*, *Music Server*, *Literature*, and *Arts*. Other self-descriptive paths provide access to the Greek Islands, mountains, rivers, and lakes, scenes of everyday life, and flora and fauna.

For additional information, see Chapter 6—Hellenic Civilization *and* Chapter 8—Hellenic Civilization.

Historical Guided Tour #1

http://www.mechan.ntua.gr/webacropol

Students can take an historical guided tour of the Acropolis and surrounding monuments, including Propylaia, the Temple of Athena Nike, the Parthenon, and the Erechtheion.

Historical Guided Tour #2

http://www.indiana.edu/~kglowack/Athens/Athens.html

The Department of Classical Studies at the University of Indiana in Bloomington has compiled dozens of dramatic photographs of archaeological and architectural landmarks of ancient Athens, such as the Agora and the Arch of Hadrian. The exhibit is arranged by chief excavated regions and monuments. There is also a great deal of text describing the ancient civilization.

GUATEMALA

http://www.ualr.edu/~degonzalez/guatemala.html

Danny Gonzalez, who works in the academic computing department of the University of Arkansas, wants to take your students on a tour of his native Guatemala. Meet a typical rural Guatemalan family, travel to the Guatemalan Indian communities (you'll be able to tell which village you're in by the type of embroidery, color, design, and shape of the local clothing), and visit the Mestizos and the "gariganus" of the Caribbean coast. Also view structures from ancient, colonial, and contemporary Guatemala, and view the country's flora and fauna. The Guatemala presented here is a happy and colorful land; Gonzalez does not address any of the unsavory political information.

http://www.artemaya.com/

The highlands of Guatemala, home to many descendants of the ancient Mayans, is one of the most beautiful areas of Central America. Your class can visit the area and meet some of the self-taught artists who live there, view their oil paintings, and read their biographies. Information, available in both English and Spanish, covers interesting aspects of the local culture. For example, the bonesetters will be more than happy to teach you how they are able to mend broken bones in no time at all using only their hands and heated tobacco leaves.

HAITI

http://pasture.ecn.purdue.edu/~agenhtml/agenmc/haiti/haiti.html

Students of Purdue University in Indiana invite you on a tour of Haiti. We took the tour and discovered that Haiti was the first republic in the world to be led by a person of African descent. We owe Jean-Jacques Dessaline our thanks—his victory over Napoleon forced the emperor to abandon his plans for control of Louisiana. In addition to learning local history and culture, the tour includes views of various Haitian landscapes, cities, and beaches. You can also listen to Haitian music, learn about voodoo, and enjoy the local cuisine. Be warned—you need good strong teeth to be able to eat griots (boiled then fried goat).

HIMALAYAS

See Chapter 3—Natural Wonders—Himalayas.

HONG KONG

http://www.cuhk.hk/pearl.htm

The Chinese University of Hong Kong will take you on a photographic tour of their country, known as the Pearl of the Orient. If you have the time, you might want to take the side trip to Tibet. It will be interesting to note what changes will occur in this site now that the Chinese have assumed control.

INDIA

See also Chapter 3—Natural Wonders—Himalayas.

Alamkara: 5,000 Years of Indian Art

http://www.ncb.gov.sg/nhb/alam

Alamkara is a Sanskrit word meaning ornamentation of decoration. The Asian Civilization Museum, National Heritage Board of Singapore, and the National New Delhi Museum have established the eight exhibits at this site, which illustrate "Alamkara" in relation to Indian culture, dress, history, and religion. The subjects in the exhibits range from kings, courtiers, and craftsmen to mortal women and celestial men.

Assam

http://www.acsu.buffalo.edu/~talukdar/assam/assamhome.html

Dipanker Talukdar, an engineering graduate student at the University of Buffalo, has produced this comprehensive site about the state of Assam. Although the organization and predominantly textual composition of this site makes it seem more like a reference book than a virtual field trip, we have included it because it's so thorough and because it has numerous links to other Indian web sites. If Talukdar has left anything out, we can't imagine what that might be. In addition to maps and information about language and literature (including translations of short stories), he has amassed data on geography, flora and fauna, history, economics, culture, travel information, current events, and even humor, although you will not get the jokes unless you have some knowledge of various Indian languages.

INUIT PEOPLE

See Canada, *above*.

IRAN

http://www.anglia.ac.uk/~trochford/isfahan.html

Take your students to Isfahan, one of ten cities designated by UNESCO as a universal heritage. We recommend that you first stop at the *Tour Shop,* where you can pick up a free map of Isfahan showing all of the city's mosques, shrines, minarets, palaces, and bridges. If your students aren't too impatient, stay a bit longer and obtain a copy of the *Fundamental Concepts*, a primer on Islamic architecture. Then it's off on your tour, hosted by a professor at Britain's Anglia Polytech University, who will explain the relationship between Islam, architecture, and history while showing you stunning interiors and exteriors of buildings.

IRAQ

See Arab Countries, *above*.

ISRAEL

See also Chapter 3—Natural Wonders—Deserts.

http://www1.huji.ac.il/jeru/jerusalem.html

Your class can travel the city of Jerusalem, both Old and New, through different periods of time, meet the people, taste the food, see special costumes, visit local sites, and see portraits, old maps, landscapes, and works of art. The site is hosted by the Israeli government, so for a complete unit on the Middle East, you may want to balance this trip with other materials.

JAPAN

See also Chapter 3—Aquatic and Marine Life—Enoshima Aquarium, *and* Kaiyukan Aquarium; Chapter 5—Theater—Kabuki Theater; *and* Chapter 11—Schools—Japan.

National Museum of Japanese History

http://trisun.rekihaku.ac.jp/rekihaku/index.html

This institution, located in Rekihaku, is Japan's only nationally operated history museum. Exhibits cover the full spectrum of Japanese history and culture, from the Paleolithic era to modern times. Various moments of history and scenes of every day life are portrayed through images and artifacts. Information is available in both English and Japanese.

On-line Guided Tour

http://jw.stanford.edu/KIDS/kids_home.html

This tour of Japan for primary grade students is hosted by Stanford University. In addition to on-line story books and a picture dictionary in English and Japanese, which can be read or heard, students can visit a restaurant or a local school. The restaurant has a menu with a pronunciation guide. Inside the school your students can learn Hiragana, Katakana, and Kanji. They can also visit the arts and crafts classes and learn origami.

Shizuoka and Mt. Fuji

http://www.jnto.go.jp/05regional/Shizuoka/05frame.html

Visit Shizuoka, located in the approximate geographic center of Japan and best known for Mt. Fuji. In addition to Mt. Fuji, you will be able to see hot springs, the southern Japanese Alps, Nihondaira, Shiraito Falls, shrines, ruins, castles, and sand dunes. While you're there, be sure to attend some of the local festivals and learn all about green tea and tea ceremonies.

Tokugawa Art Museum

http://www.cjn.or.jp/tokugawa/index.html

Take your students to the Tokugawa Art Museum in Ngoya, Japan. Although the usual admission is 100 yen, plus plane fare, your visit will be free of charge via the Internet. This institution, the third oldest privately endowed museum in Japan, preserves the holdings of the Owari branch of the Tokugawa family, who maintained the closest family and political ties to the ruling shoguns throughout the Edo period (1603-1868). At the core of the collection are objects inherited from the first shogun, Ieyasu. The collection includes 8 *Designated National Treasures*, 50 *Registered Important Cultural Properties*, and 44 *Important Art Objects*, such as warrior saddles and armor from the sixteenth century, mirrors and chests from the private rooms of a shogun, a traditional Noh theater stage and masks, and tea ceremonial objects. Narratives accompany each image. Visitors can also see the museum grounds and garden tea houses.

JORDAN

See also Arab Countries, *above.*

http://www.arabia.com/Jordan

Visit some of the famous sites of Jordan, such as Petra—the 2,000-year-old rock carved city—and the Dead Sea, where students can see photographs of the Jordan River. (Be prepared for a disappointment—the Jordan River is surprisingly small. Henry Kissinger, upon seeing it, remarked, "It's amazing what PR can do for a little river.") While traveling, learn about Jordan's history, geography, culture, cuisine, and holidays.

KUWAIT

See Arab Countries, *above.*

LAOS

See Thailand, *below.*

LEBANON

See Arab Countries, *above.*

MEXICO

http://mexico.udg.mx/ingles.html

This tour of Mexico is sponsored by the University of Guadalajara. The tour includes information about and photographs of local history, geography, art, and cuisine. Materials are available in both Spanish and English.

MOROCCO

See Arab Countries, *above*.

MYANMAR

See also Cambodia, *above; and* Chapter 3—Natural Wonders—Himalayas.

http://www.myanmar.com

Anything you want to know about Myanmar can be found in this government-sponsored site, including photographs of traditional puppets and architectural drawings of famous temples. You can even take a field trip down the Ayeawaddy River, the only river in southeast Asia completely contained within one country. Because this site is government sponsored, expect a sanitized view of the political and human rights situation.

NEPAL—MT. EVEREST

See also Chapter 3—Natural Wonders—Himalayas.

http://www.library.advanced.org/10131/nepal.html

Dozens of stunning photographs of the awesome mountains, valleys, plateaus, people, and bazaars, with straightforward texts that are easy to understand but highly informative. There are even short quizzes to test your knowledge. The people who put together this field trip obviously love, respect, and know Nepal.

NEW ZEALAND

http://nz.com/tour

Haere mai, haere mai! Welcome to New Zealand. Learn all about the country while touring Akaroa, the Coromondel Peninsula, Moeraki and Moeraki Boulder, the Otago Peninsula, Wellington, and the North and South Islands.

NILE RIVER

http://www.adventureonline.com/nile/index.html

Is your class ready to shoot the white waters of the Nile River, near its headwaters in Uganda? Join a team of kayakers—read their journal entries, view their dramatic photographs, and send them e-mail. Along the trip your class will learn about the Nile, Uganda, and crocodiles. Follow the journey on a colorful topographic map. Several classroom activities, included on site, will help you with your planning.

NORWAY

See Chapter 4—Northern Lights Planetarium.

OMAN

See Arab Countries, *above*.

PACIFIC NORTHWEST COAST INDIANS

See also Chapter 6—Native American Art—Northwest Coast Tribal Art.

http://www.onaben.org/hstory/dirlist.html

Take your students to the rugged Pacific Northwest—the area from the Columbia River in Washington, through British Columbia and on into Alaska—to see and learn about the art, the architecture, and the ceremonial, social, and spiritual beliefs of the Pacific Northwest Coast Indians.

PAKISTAN

See Chapter 3—Natural Wonders—Himalayas.

POLAND

See Chapter 3—Botanic Gardens—Botanic Garden of Warsaw.

QATAR

See Arab Countries, *above*.

RUSSIA

See also Chapter 1—Soviet Union—Soviet Archives; Chapter 6—Pushkin Museum of Fine Arts; *and* Chapter 10—Photojournalism.

Library of Congress Soviet Archives Exhibit

http://sunsite.unc.edu/expo/soviet.exhibit/soviet.archive.html

This is the Library of Congress's Soviet archives exhibit, a collection of previously secret Soviet papers spanning the period from Lenin through the Cold War. There are so many fascinating papers in this exhibit that we can't begin to summarize them. Suffice to say that whether you're studying Soviet or United States history, Communism, labor unions, or any wars even indirectly involving the Soviet Union since 1917, you will want to visit this exhibit.

See also Chapter 1—Soviet Union—Soviet Archives *for additional descriptions of this site.*

On-line Tour

http://www.cs.toronto.edu/~mes/russia

A tour of Moscow, St. Petersburg, Karelia, northwest Russia, central Russia, south Russia, Ural, Siberia, and far east Russia is available from this site. See current and historic photographs, maps, flags, and local people and customs. There is even a map of the Moscow subway system. Like Russia itself, this site is so diverse and huge that you may wish to utilize the on-site search function. For example, we entered "weather" and found, among other things, a place where we could obtain current weather conditions in various parts of Russia.

Window to Russia

http://www.wtr.ru

Window to Russia, a Moscow-based project by Relcom Corporation, provides access to a variety of information resources from and about Russia. Hosts have provided an interactive Russian-English dictionary because some of the resources are available only in Russian. Materials include information and images of Soviet documents, Victor Bogorad (St. Petersburg's top cartoonist), and detailed information about Russia. There is also a direct link to the Paleontology Institute of the Russian Academy of Science. The academy is the world's largest paleontology museum, and the site was developed to create an on-line exhibition of Mongolian dinosaurs and Pleistocene and Tertiary mammals.

SAUDI ARABIA

See Arab Countries, *above*.

SINGAPORE

Museum of Singapore Art and History

http://www.museum.org.sg

Five separate museums take you on a tour of Asian civilizations and Singapore art, history, and historical documents.

See also Chapter 8—Museum of Singapore Art and History.

SOVIET UNION

See Russia, *above.*

SPAIN

http://www.DocuWeb.ca/SiSpain

The Spanish Embassy in Canada has provided this interactive service to "promote the free exchange of information on Spanish current affairs and its historical, linguistic, and cultural development." There is extensive information on virtually every topic, including geography, demographics, history, language, culture, politics, economics, infrastructure, and government. If you want to learn Spanish, they will direct you to appropriate Internet sites. The entire site can be read in either English or Spanish.

SUDAN

See Arab Countries, *above.*

SYRIA

See Arab Countries, *above.*

TAIWAN

http://www.npm.gov.tw

The National Palace Museum of Taiwan has an extensive collection of paintings and calligraphy dating from the fourth century. The works are on paper and silk, and exposure to the light and air hastens their aging process and eventual ruin. As a result, the works are only on display for three-month intervals. However, you can view them year round at this site. Accompanying texts are available in English or Taiwanese.

THAILAND

http://www.asiatour.com/thailand/content1.htm

Take your students on a field trip to Thailand where they will be able to attend various festivals, see the country and its people and sites, and watch video clips. The site allows students to prepare for their trip by studying entry regulations, currency, health, transportation, and cuisine. You might want to check the "Map Room" for detailed maps of Thailand and nearby countries. Tours of Cambodia, Laos, Myanmar, Vietnam, and Yunnan are also available.

TIBET

See Chapter 3—Natural Wonders—Himalayas.

TUNISIA

See Arab Countries, *above*.

TURKEY

http://www.turkishnews.com/DiscoverTurkey

Although this tour is conducted from a strongly partisan Turkish point of view, there is still much to see and do during your travels. Tour guides will cover Turkish history, carpets, culture, and government and even play the Turkish National Anthem and Mozart's *Turkish March*. You may wish to bypass information about Cyprus, as well as the first highlighted section of this site, which proclaims how the new Greek government sponsors international terrorism.

UGANDA

See Nile River, *above*.

UNITED ARAB EMIRATES

See Arab Countries, *above*.

UNITED KINGDOM

See also Chapter 3—Aquatic and Marine Life—Underwater Guide.

Tower of London

http://www.voicenet.com/~dravyk/toltour

Tour Europe's oldest palace, fortress, and prison. Your tour begins with the Tower as it stands today, complete with the day and time in London at the precise moment you log in, and views of flightless ravens. You are then taken back in time to the Tower's beginnings. The tour works its way forward in time and, in the process, digresses to cover famous people connected in one way or another with the Tower, such as William the Conqueror, Richard II, Richard III, Walter Raleigh, Anne Boleyn, Guy Fawkes, and of course, King Henry.

Welsh Castles

http://www.castlewales.com/home.html

Your class can visit over 100 Welsh castles and abbeys. Jeff Thomas, a castle enthusiast, will escort you on the tour and provide information that imparts a genuine feeling for what life inside a castle was really like. For example, Thomas explains such things as the ingenious construction of fireplaces and how they were designed to spread heat the maximum distance. He also covers pre-castle Welsh history and provides an historical timeline, a glossary, and a bibliography.

UNITED STATES

Alaska

See also Pacific Northwest Coast Indians, *above;* Chapter 5—Sports and Sporting Events—Dog Sledding; *and* Chapter 11—Schools—United States—Alaska.

http://www.AlaskaOne.com/travel/alaska.html

Visit Alaska's natural wonders, its wildlife and humans, from the tundra to the mountains. This sprawling site features beautiful photographs and a wealth of information about Alaska's present and past. If you can't find what you're looking for here, there are numerous links to other sites.

California—Alcatraz Island

http://www.nps.gov/alcatraz

Follow the pelican icon provided on site for an Alcatraz Island tour conducted by the United States National Park Service. Alcatraz, originally known as La Isla de los Alcatracas (pelicans), has had many identities and functions through the centuries. Students may be especially interested in the *Frequently Asked Questions* (FAQ) section, which answers such questions as the location of the cells of Al Capone and the famous Birdman, and why the penitentiary was closed.

See also Chapter 8—Indians of the Americas.

California—Golden Gate Bridge

http://www2.goldengate.org/goldengate

Your class can tour one of the most famous and romantic bridges in the United States with the Golden Gate Bridge Highway and Transportation District. They will be able to see photographs of the bridge as it stands today and as it was being built while they learn interesting facts. For example, as late as 1916, engineers insisted that it would be impossible to construct the bridge. It was only due to the dreams and perseverance of one man, Joseph Baermann, that the Golden Gate Bridge exists. In addition to a detailed history—political, engineering, and financial—of the bridge, there is also a list of answers to frequently asked questions. Do you know why the bridge was painted orange rather than gold? Learn about the seismic retrofitting project and catch up on the most recent news releases about the bridge.

California Living Museum

See Chapter 3—Zoos, Farms, and Animals.

California—Los Angeles River

http://www.lalc.k12.ca.us/laep/smart/river/tour

The high school student who created this site tells us that many people have never heard of the Los Angeles River. Therefore, he created this site, which allows you to digitally navigate this 50-mile river from its headwaters in the San Fernando Valley to its mouth in Long Beach. Along the way you can view the local sights, plants, animals, and architecture, while learning about history.

California Redwood Canyons

See Chapter 3—Natural Wonders—California Redwood Canyons.

Florida

See Chapter 3—Aquatic and Marine Life—Florida Aquarium *and* Parks and Sanctuaries—Corkscrew Swamp Sanctuary.

Hawaii—Oahu

See also Chapter 3—Aquatic and Marine Life—Scuba Diving in Maui.

http://www.hcc.hawaii.edu/hawaii

Take a tour of Oahu, courtesy of Hawaii Community College. There are over 75 photographs of Oahu and its environs, with very brief accompanying text.

Illinois—Chicago—Chicago Historical Society

See Chapter 8—Chicago Historical Society.

Illinois—Chicago—Chicago Stock Exchange

http://www.chicagostockex.com

The wheelers and dealers at the Chicago Stock Exchange can't help trying to get you to invest in stocks. However, if you can resist the sales pitch, there is a lot to learn during your visit, including the history of and facts about the exchange as well as an historical photographic tour.

Illinois—Illinois State Museum

See Chapter 8—Illinois State Museum.

Louisiana

See Chapter 3—Bird Watching—Birds of Southwestern Louisiana.

Massachusetts—Massachusetts Tide Pool

See Chapter 3—Aquatic and Marine Life—Massachusetts Tide Pool.

Massachusetts—Nantucket Island

See Chapter 11—Schools—United States—Massachusetts.

Mississippi—Oxford

See Chapter 12—Faulkner, William.

Missouri—St. Louis

http://www.nps.gov/jeff/arch-home/index.htm

Pay a visit to the St. Louis arch. There are several interesting facts and narratives as well as photographs showing the construction and current pictures of the arch. Students will even find equations used in calculating the curve and learn the importance of the "keystone" in arch construction.

New England—Covered Bridges

http://william-king.www.drexel.edu/top/bridge/cb1.html

Roger McCain, a professor of economics at Drexel University, wants to take your students on a tour of the covered bridges of southeastern Pennsylvania, New Jersey, Maryland, and Delaware. McCain sees the old "kissing bridges" as a reminder of a time "when life was simpler and closer to the land," and his love for the bridges is evident. Your students may wonder why bridges were covered—McCain explains. Students can choose tours either by county or structural type. We recommend the *Photographic Essay* section, which combines historical data and local lore. There are images of covered bridges in every season, as well as links to other bridge sites that delve deeper into engineering data.

New York—Buffalo Zoological Gardens

See Chapter 3—Zoos, Farms, and Animals.

New York—Central Park

http://www.centralpark.org/home.html

New York's Central Park was the first landscaped park in the United States. There are more than 50 places to explore on this self-guided tour, including the park's zoos, statues, and gardens. Learn about the history of Central Park and participate in a sport of your choice—we suggest lawn bowling. If you tire of wandering the park's several hundred acres, sit back and watch the video.

New York City Ballet

See Chapter 5—Ballet.

Ohio—Wright Patterson Air Force Base

See Chapter 9—Science—Museums—Aviation and Aerospace.

Oregon, The Bridges of

http://www.teleport.com/~bizave/portland/bridges

The first bridge across the Willamette River was constructed in 1887. Since that time, approximately two dozen other automobile and railroad bridges have been constructed across the Willamette and Columbia Rivers. Students can view the various bridges and learn about their construction while learning some interesting Pacific Northwest history.

Texas

See Chapter 3—Aquatic and Marine Life—Lake Big Fish *and* Chapter 11—Schools—United States—Texas.

Virginia—University of Virginia

http://www.virginia.edu/about.html

Thomas Jefferson considered the founding of the University of Virginia and the design of many of its buildings and grounds one of his greatest accomplishments. The institution is noted for its distinctive grounds and buildings, particularly for the section known as *The Lawn*. On this page under "Information for Visitors to the University," students can tour the gardens, rotunda, and ten pavilions that compose this area while learning about classical architecture and history.

See also Chapter 12—Jefferson, Thomas.

Washington

See Pacific Northwest Coast Indians, *above*.

Washington, D.C.—Library of Congress

See Chapter 10—Library of Congress.

Washington, D.C.—National Archives and Records Administration

See Chapter 8—National Archives and Records Administration.

Washington, D.C.—On-line Tour

http://sc94.ameslab.gov/TOUR/tour.html

Take your students on a tour of our nation's capital. Detailed maps of the city and its subway system are provided, along with directions to each of the attractions. Your students will be able to see and read about such landmarks and cultural institutions as the Jefferson Memorial, Ford Theater, the Federal Bureau of Investigation, and the Lincoln Memorial.

Washington, D.C.—United States House of Representatives and Senate

http://www.house.gov

Students can visit Congress and learn about the legislative process, about who's who in the House of Representatives, and how to contact congressmen by e-mail or "snail mail." Those interested in current events will be able to find the latest updates on pending bills and amendments. Your class can also pay a visit to the Senate at http://www.senate.gov.

Washington, D.C.—White House

http://www.whitehouse.gov/WH/Welcome-nt.html

Pay a visit to the president, his family, and the White House. Click on photographs of the president, the vice-president, and their families for biographical information, copies of speeches, and e-mail addresses. You can travel from room to room in the White House, and in each room you will find information on history, furnishings, and current happenings. The Virtual Library contains documents dating back to the start of the Clinton administration, including transcripts of the president's radio addresses and executive orders. Stop by the Briefing Room for the day's press releases and the most up-to-date federal statistics. Socks the Cat will also take children on his own White House tour, talking about other pets and kids who have inhabited his current home. There is also a quarterly newsletter, *Inside the White House*, which addresses such topics as crime, drugs, and poverty, in language geared towards grade-school children. Some of the newsletters are directly from the president, and others are from members of his administration.

Wyoming

See Chapter 11—Schools—United States—Wyoming.

UNITED STATES MILITARY AGENCIES

See also Chapter 9—Science—Museums—Aviation and Aerospace.

Coast Guard

http://www.dot.gov/dotinfo/uscg

This award-winning official U.S. Coast Guard site has biographies, speeches, and information about the Coast Guard commandant, information about the Coast Guard's role in the 1996 summer Olympics, photographs, drawings, maps, and vessel and aircraft data sheets. The site is updated weekly with information about and pictures of the latest Coast Guard operations. Younger students will want to visit the *Kid's Corner,* which has an on-line coloring book with water safety tips and an audio recording of the Coast Guard anthem.

Department of the Air Force

http://www.af.mil

This official U.S. Air Force site contains current Air Force news and information, fact sheets, a career center, and biographies of Air Force leaders. Pay a visit to the library, where you will find not only information about the Air Force bands but also sound clips of several songs, including *Hail to the Chief.* There is also an exhibition of photographs and paintings depicting space exploration, various planes, and Air Force personnel and legendary figures.

VIETNAM

See also Thailand, *above;* Chapter 5—Theater—Miss Saigon; *and* Chapter 10—Photojournalism.

http://www.vietvet.org/visit.htm

Vietnam veterans will take your students on a tour of Vietnam and share their views of the changes that have transpired in the country since the war. For example, Special Forces veteran Bob Donoghu will take them into the hills as he makes his first humanitarian assistance trip to the Bru tribe. The vets' observations about Vietnam range from reminiscences to tips for travelers, such as, "Be nice to the kids who harass you for sodas and gum—and be thankful that your own children do not have to do that to support you or themselves."

YEMEN

See Arab Countries, *above*.

YUNNAN

See Thailand, *above*.

CHAPTER 3

The Natural World

From whales to gnats, from the bottom of the ocean floor to the pinnacles of the Himalayas, from the barren Negev Desert to lush botanical gardens—your students can spend the day viewing nature's wonders. Spend a few hours at the world's zoos, look at the world through the eyes of a bee, fly through the eye of a hurricane, or perform a virtual frog dissection.

AQUATIC AND MARINE LIFE

The Amazing Fish Cam

http://www.netscape.com/fishcam/fishcam.html

How would you like your own maintenance-free classroom aquarium? Simply connect to the *Amazing Fish Cam* where you can take a "real-time" view of a 90-gallon tank filled with eels and other sea life. A picture is taken every 60 seconds and transferred to the Internet. The best part is that you never have to feed the fish or clean the tank.

Enoshima Aquarium

http://www.iseshima.com/enoshima/index.html

The Enoshima Aquarium in Japan has a collection of local and worldwide marine life. Taking your students to a foreign aquarium affords a unique perspective. For example, a collection of photos showing people touching some of the fish and dolphins carries this caption: "To become familiar with animals promotes the nurturing of the emotions and it provides a very good influence in character building, especially for children. Many kinds of efforts are being made so that the visitors . . . feel a kind of skin contact."

Florida Aquarium

http://www.sptimes.com/aquarium

The Florida Aquarium exhibits marine life in unique, native settings. Let the *St. Petersburg Times* newspaper take your students on a tour of natural habitats where they will be able to follow the life cycle of a drop of water through a local mangrove forest, out to the bays and beaches, by the coral reef, to offshore—all while visiting and learning about local wildlife. They will be able to participate in experiments for "wannabe marine biologists of all ages" and obtain information on marine residents through an "open channel to aquarium experts." There is also a *Play Pond* in the *Swamp of Knowledge* where knowledge of natural Florida can be tested, as well as such games as *Critter Match* where pictures are matched with facts.

Great White Shark

http://www.cybervault.com/users/D/dgrgich/shark.html

No trip to the seas would be complete without an encounter with the Great White Shark. Your students will probably want to see the close-up view of a shark's jaws, as well as the photograph of a great white swimming near an unprotected diver. Every documented attack by a great white is listed, and the "shark attack capital of the world" is identified.

Kaiyukan Aquarium

http://www.hitachizosen.co.jp/info/kaiyukan/kaiyukan-e.html

The Kaiyukan Aquarium in Japan recreates the diverse environment found along the Ring of Fire, the world's active volcanic and earthquake belt. Begin your tour in a Japanese forest above the water's surface and gradually descend, circumventing the Pacific Ocean.

Lake Big Fish

http://www.cirr.com/~gensie

Lake Big Fish in Plano, Texas, which is more of a suburban pond than an actual lake, has been certified as a "Backyard Habitat" by the National Wildlife Federation. Your students may see the lake in summer, fall, winter, and spring and learn about the birds and other wildlife and the honeysuckle and other plant life. Urban, suburban, and rural students will learn that nature can be found and appreciated even in unlikely places.

Lamont-Doherty Earth Observatory

http://www.ldeo.columbia.edu/us_margins

This site is hosted by Columbia University's Lamont-Doherty Earth Observatory. Students can see images of the sea floor off of the U.S. coast and read the results of observatory research. The images and explanatory texts, which include information on underwater caves and giant salt fields, are powerful. As one scientist points out, "The sea floor off the U.S. coast is as remarkable and . . . as alien as landscapes we've seen on Mars and Venus."

Los Angeles River

See Chapter 2—United States—California—Los Angeles River.

Massachusetts Tide Pool

http://www.umassd.edu/Public/People/Kamaral/thesis/tidepools.html

Learn all about the plants and creatures residing in a typical Massachusetts tide pool. Kimberly Amaral, a graduate student at Dartmouth and science writer for CompuServe, has put her thesis on the Internet. A map of a tide pool appears, and students can click on any organism of interest, from arthropods to sea urchins. There are also projects for working with tide pool flora, such as making seaweed prints. Surely, home economics teachers will appreciate the recipe for seaweed pudding.

Nile River

See Chapter 2—Nile River.

Ocean Planet Online

http://seawifs.gsfc.nasa.gov/ocean_planet.html

The National Aeronautics and Space Administration's *Ocean Planet Online* is an exhibition that examines the diversity of and environmental issues faced by the world's oceans. The exhibition is organized around an interactive floor plan of the Smithsonian Institution's Ocean Planet traveling exhibition and includes text, graphic, audio, and video materials. Students have a choice of taking a guided tour of the exhibit or conducting keyword searches for specific topics. There is also a resource page, access to educational materials, and teacher resources.

Scuba Diving in Maui

http://www.maui.net/~scuba/index.html

What better way to learn about underwater life than through scuba diving? An interactive map allows you to learn about various diving sites in Maui through descriptions and pictures. Hosts have thought of just about everything, including detailed reports of weather and sea conditions to insure a safe dive. They will teach you how to take underwater photographs. If you don't want to lug all that heavy equipment, they'll be more than happy to share their own photographs with you through a slide show that displays such underwater life as Moorish idols and thread fin butterfly fish.

Sea World

http://www.bev.net/education/SeaWorld/homepage.html

Your students can take a virtual tour of Sea World and learn about and view animals and marine life. You can even send e-mail questions to Shamu, and he promises to respond. In addition to excellent pictures of aquatic animals with accompanying text, there are downloadable teacher guides and information on careers in marine mammal science. *Animal Quiz* lets you click on a sound and try to match it with the correct animal. There is also a section called *Fun Facts*, but the facts don't seem all that much fun. For example, a fun fact about the carpet python is that "pythons have vestigial or leftover pelvic girdles and hind limbs that show up externally as a pair of spurs near the base of the tail."

Smithsonian Institution Underwater Pictures

http://www.actwin.com/fish/pictures/smithsonian.html

The Smithsonian Institution has compiled 13 pictures and brief texts of dolphins, coral, crabs, cuttlefish, anemones, and other creatures and habitats.

Turtle Trax

See Zoos, Farms, and Animals, *below*.

Underwater Guide

http://www.gla.ac.uk/~gbza62/contents.html

This site takes you to the seas of the United Kingdom as well as to the Red Sea. Although there is virtually no text, there are dozens of stunning photos of fish and other marine life.

Whale Watching

http://vvv.com/ai/demos/whale.html

This interactive site teaches students to identify whales through a series of responses to on-line questions and moving images. Answers are automatically scored.

WhaleNet

http://whale.wheelock.edu

WhaleNet, one of the most complete Internet information sources on whales, was developed jointly by the biology departments of Wheelock and Simmons Colleges and the National Science Foundation. Students can learn about whale tagging and tracking by satellites. They can download maps showing migratory patterns or download blank maps and recorded sightings and create their own map. *WhaleNet* also has information and bibliographies on every species of whale. If you don't find the information you need, you can e-mail questions to on-line scientists. Teachers may want to visit this site ahead of time and download the species identification chart.

Whale's World

http://fas.sfu.ca/cs/research/whales

The *Virtual Whale's World Project* from Simon Fraser University in Canada, is intended to be "an education and conservation tool to celebrate the lives of humpback whales." Sounds and 3-D animations enable visitors to hear and see the feeding behaviors of Pacific humpback whales. There is also dramatic underwater footage. The text on how pods of humpbacks trap and feed on schools of herrings should leave no doubt in anyone's mind about the intelligence of whales.

BIRD WATCHING

Birds of Fermilab

http://www.fnal.gov/ecology/wildlife/list.html

Fermilab is a world-famous high energy physics laboratory located in suburban Chicago. In addition to contributing to the world of science, Fermilab is also interested in preserving nature. The facility's 6,800 acres of grounds contain a myriad of aviary life, which is available for viewing on site. See and obtain information about such varied life as the great white pelican, the Canada goose, the wood duck, and the American Wigeon. You don't have to worry about getting lost on the grounds because the laboratory provides a detailed map.

Birds of Southwestern Louisiana

http://www.ucs.usl.edu/~pec8774

Take your students for a bird-watching field trip in southwestern Louisiana. There are photographs and information on over 250 native species and bird-watching sites.

Sandpiper and Plover Migration

http://www.utm.edu/~phertzel/migration.htm

This site provides current information on the sandpiper and plover migration through the lower 48 states. Students can select a particular species (there are dozens of choices) from an on-site list and follow it to a U.S. map that tracks the birds' actual migration pattern. They may also report their own sightings via e-mail or telephone and view vivid photographs.

BOTANIC GARDENS

Australian Botanic Gardens

http://155.187.10.12/anbg/anbg.html

See and learn about plants native to Australia, the use of plants by Australian Aboriginals, frogs and common birds (with drawings and sound), and how to grow various Australian plants.

Niagara Park Botanic Garden

http://www.npbg.org

Niagara Park, right by the Horseshoe Falls, has a botanic garden and butterfly conservatory. Pick up your copy of their magazine, *Wings and Waterfalls*, while you're there, and if you have time, wander aroung the various plants, visit with some local students, and follow their links to see the famous waterfalls.

INSECTS

See also Chapter 9—Science—Museums—General—"The Yuckiest Site on the Internet."

Ant Hill

See Chapter 13—Ant Hill.

Bee Eye

http://cvs.anu.edu.au/andy/beye/beyehome.html

B Eye allows you to see the world through the eyes of a honeybee. The site allows you to hover at close range or get a "full-scope" view.

Bee Research Center

http://198.22.133.109

The people at the Carl Hayden Bee Research Center, sponsored by the United States Department of Agriculture, have some bee-yootiful photos and a lot of information on bees they would like to share with you and your students. On the home page, students can read, "Why Is That Bee Giving Me the Raspberries?" and find out that it is nothing personal on the part of the bee. Lest they begin to feel too comfortable, there is also an article on the disturbing behavior of the African killer honeybee. There is a link on the home page to *The Internet Classroom,* which, although implying lesson plans, delivers one interesting activity and a lot more information. The activity illustrates the surprising fact that four out of every five bites of food we take is the direct result of pollination. (Researchers may be out of touch with the junk food diet, however.) *The Internet Classroom* is divided into adult and K-12 activities, but there is little difference in the tone or presentation, so check both sections. Students will learn how honeybee workers find flowers and then return to the hive and "dance" to let their friends know where the flowers are. The section *Trivial Pursuits* contains interesting facts about bees and may be used as a handout. There is also a section that describes how bees see the world around them, but for an actual visual experience, see the site listed above.

The Bug Club

http://www.ex.ac.uk/bugclub

This award-winning site, hosted by students in the biology department at the University of Exeter in the United Kingdom, is a "club run for children and the young at heart who are interested in bugs and other creepy crawlies." The biology students will share articles, photographs, bug care sheets, games, and puzzles. A clickable bug hunt is currently under construction. Students can also find pen pals and make nominations for "bug of the week."

Bugs You Want in Your Computer

http://bugwatch.com/bugindex.html

This cleverly titled site is a photographic essay covering ants, butterflies, wasps, bees, dragonflies, flies, bugs, mantids, hoppers, beetles, cicadas, and spiders.

Entomology Image Gallery

http://www.ent.iastate.edu/imagegallery

The Department of Entomology at Iowa State University has dozens of pictures and movies about ticks, beetles, mosquitoes, lice, and other insects common to the Midwest. We're certain that your class will enjoy the sequence of pictures that show "the dissecting of the midgut from a partially engorged adult female deer tick." For anyone who's ever been tormented by mosquitoes, here's a chance to watch scientists return the favor.

Furman University Insect Collection

http://www.furman.edu/~snyder/butterfly/index.html

Visit the Biology Department at Furman University in Greenville, South Carolina, to see their collection of moth and butterfly images. Although most of the butterflies in the collection are Lepidoptera, there are other species primarily from the southeastern United States.

Richard B. Dominick Moth and Butterfly Collection

http://zebra.biol.scarolina.edu/moth.html

Richard B. Dominick's moth and butterfly collection, located on the Columbia Campus of South Carolina, has over 26,000 specimens representing over 11,000 species collected between 1965 and 1975. The specimens were collected at the Wedge Plantation, a varied environment with rice fields, cypress swamps, and a pine and hardwood forest.

NATURAL WONDERS

California Redwood Canyons

http://redwoods.com/~ebarnett/redwood.canyons.html#intro

The Redwoods Canyon Association doesn't have a lot to say about the biology or history of the California redwoods, but they do have a lot of nice photographs, and they're certainly friendly folks, so you may want to introduce them to your students. Although most of the information is for people planning a trip to the canyons, it is all related so genially that the virtual trip is worthwhile. And, sprinkled in among the commercialism are some interesting facts. Jack London described California's Redwood Canyons as "the most unthinkably glorious body of timber to be found anywhere," but he didn't know that the biomass density of the redwood forest, according to the association, is nine times greater than that of the Amazon rain forest.

Deserts

http://environment.negev.k12.il/desert/deseng.htm

The desert and desertification project originated in the High School for Environment Studies in the Negev Desert in Israel. As part of an Internet project, students around the world wrote about their local desert life, scenery, and culture. This site contains the students' work as well as articles on the ancient spice route, the Dead Sea, the highland region, the Eilat mountains, and desert flowers and wildlife.

Himalayas

http://aleph0.clarku.edu/rajs/Shangri_La.html

This tour takes you to the Himalayan Range and its vicinity, which spans the northern rim of Myanmar along India, Bhutan, Nepal, and Tibet to Pakistan and Afghanistan. You can view individual peaks and pinnacles or the entire range—including the star, Mt. Everest.

Rainforests

http://sunsite.doc.ic.ac.uk/netspedition

Netspedition, hosted by Imperial College in the United Kingdom, is an interactive scientific expedition to the Amazon rainforest, which ended in late 1996. A team of research scientists conducted experiments involving such phenomena as the Amazon River, butterflies, and snakes. The expedition's methodology, some photographs, and results are posted on site, as are students' e-mail questions to scientists from around the world. In turn, students around the world can e-mail questions to the scientists. This is fundamentally a serious scientific expedition—scientists around the world, participating in the same things as students, also sent the research team questions and requests—so occasionally the information is fairly technical and rigorous. At the same time, much information is formatted with students in mind. For example, the methodology of taking periodic depth measurements of the Amazon, as "soberly" described in the posting, is to use a rope with knots of one-meter intervals.

PARKS AND SANCTUARIES

See also Volcanoes, *below.*

Central Park

See Chapter 2—United States—New York—Centeral Park.

Corkscrew Swamp Audubon Sanctuary

http://www.naples-online.com/attract/pp10-3.htm

The Corkscrew Swamp Sanctuary near Naples, Florida, contains 11,000 acres of swamps, marshes, and pine forests. The Audubon Society hosts this tour of the sanctuary's natural flora and fauna. Simply follow the wooden signposts.

Devil's Tower National Monument

See Chapter 11—Schools—United States—Wyoming.

Flaming Gorge National Recreation Area

See Chapter 11—Schools—United States—Wyoming.

Grand Canyon National Park

http://www.kaibab.org

Referring to the Grand Canyon, President Theodore Roosevelt once said: "Do nothing to mar its grandeur for the ages have been at work upon it and man cannot improve it. Keep it for your children, your children's children, and all who come after you." But he never imagined that it could be preserved and presented over the Internet, so that millions of people could view it from their homes and schools. Your students can take a guided tour of the park, complete with maps, history, scenic photographs and articles. They can also learn how to become junior rangers and how to make split twig figurines—works of art dating back 4,000 years to the forebearers of the Anasazi culture.

Grand Teton National Park

See Chapter 11—Schools—United States—Wyoming.

John Muir Trail

http://neon.cchem.berkeley.edu/~krempl/JMT.html

Dr. Stefan Krempl, an international chemist and avid outdoorsman, takes your class on a walk along the John Muir Trail from Tuolowme

Meadows in Yosemite to Mt. Whitney. The site is short on text but has stunning photographs.

For information about John Muir, see Chapter 12—Muir, John.

Oregon Trail

See Chapter 11—Schools—United States—Wyoming.

Sequoia and Kings Canyon National Park

http://www.nps.gov/seki/index.htm

The second oldest national park in the United States was established in 1890 to protect trees in the Great Forest. Students can visit the park and view such natural wonders as the General Sherman Tree, the world's largest living thing, and Mt. Whitney, the highest mountain in the United States outside of Alaska. The tour is hosted by the National Park Service.

Yellowstone National Park

See also Chapter 11—Schools—United States—Wyoming.

http://www.nps.gov/htdocs2/yell/index.htm

Pay a visit to Yellowstone National Park and view the park's natural wonders, such as geysers, trees, and Yellowstone Falls. For additional photos, see http://www.forestry.umt.edu/yellowstone.

Yosemite National Park

http://www.nps.gov/yose/yo_visit.htm

Yosemite National Park encompasses 747,956 acres and ranges in elevation from 2,000 to 13,000 feet. Students can view the sites of this national park and acquire both general and trivial knowledge from the National Park Service. For example, 2,250,000 meals are served each year by the concession stands, including 100,000 gallons of milk; 275,000 hamburgers, and 2.4 million eggs.

To see historic photographs of Yosemite, see Chapter 11—Schools—Germany—Patch American High School—Stuttgart, Germany.

VOLCANOES

Michigan Tech University

http://www.geo.mtu.edu/volcanoes

Michigan Tech University, in cooperation with the Keweenaw Volcano Observatory, has compiled an ongoing data base of current and historic volcanic activity for every volcanic range on Earth, including satellite and ground photographs. Other available materials include articles on volcanic research, remote sensing, safety tips, and the eruptive products. There is even a section on volcano humor, which, as you might expect, is quite short.

Volcano World

http://volcano.und.nodak.edu

Volcano World contains high-quality remote sensing images, interactive experiments, and comprehensive information on volcanoes. Visit volcanoes of the world, the moon, and Mars; see what's erupting at the current time; learn how to build a model and become a volcanologist; and visit volcanic parks and monuments.

WEATHER

The Cloud Boutique

http://vortex.plymouth.edu/clouds.html

Those who no longer have the available time or surroundings to lie in a field and watch the clouds roll across the sky will want to visit The Weather Center at New Hampshire's Plymouth College. Watch beautiful photographs of the various kinds of clouds and cloud formations, with detailed texts on each. There is also a 30-minute time-lapse video loop showing how clouds move and change shape.

Hurricane Storm Science Center

http://www.miamisci.org/hurricane

Students can learn about and use tools for measuring air pressure, weather conditions, moisture, etc. The site also takes you inside a hurricane, where you can learn how hurricanes work and see and learn about planes that fly through them. See actual photos of hurricanes, such as Andrew, in 3-D and learn how to make a hurricane spiral. *Killer Storms* will teach students about hurricane tracking, storm warnings, safety rules, and how to make a hurricane shopping list. The *Healing Quilt* allows people to share stories of weather disasters.

On-line Guide to Meteorology

http://ww2010.atmos.uiuc.edu

The University of Illinois has compiled this extensive guide that covers all facets of weather and meteorological phenomena. Students can visit the *Cloud Catalog* and learn about various types of clouds and how they are formed. There is also a glossary and various student activities, such as the "cloud in a bottle experiment." *Atmospheric Pressure* introduces the concept of pressure and how it varies with height, the importance of isobars, and how these concepts are necessary for the understanding of cyclones and wind generation. *Atmospheric Optics* introduces the concepts of refraction, reflection, diffraction, and the scattering of light and the optical effects that result from rainbows. A gallery of optical effects is included. *Forces and Winds* introduces the pressure gradient and coriaolis forces and their role in wind generation, and *Guide to Fronts* investigates warm, cold, stationary, and occluded fronts. Other sections deal with weather maps and images, hurricanes, land-sea breezes, and lake effect snow. There is a large collection of slides and accompanying text that investigates thunderstorms and thunderstorm phenomena, such as tornadoes, hail, and damaging winds, as well as a special case study that includes images from tornado footage. Many of the sections of this site have student activities and experiments.

University of Illinois Weather Machine

gopher://wx.atmos.uiuc.edu

The University of Illinois *Weather Machine* is one of the most popular weather sites on the Internet. Students can get up-to-the-minute weather reports for anywhere in the United States, as well as the Caribbean and Canada, by clicking on an interactive weather map. There are also satellite images, dozens of articles on weather and weather-related phenomena, dangerous weather safety tips, and much more.

ZOOS, FARMS, AND ANIMALS

Birmingham Zoo

http://www.traveller.com/zoo

The virtual Birmingham Zoo includes straightforward information about and pictures of animals. Although the collection is limited to the usual animals, you can go the Animal Omnibus section, where, by choosing any of the dozens of animals listed, you can link to other sites on the World Wide Web. However, the zoo does not check these pages, so you might want to scout them in advance. The zookeepers take annual trips to such places as the Galapagos Islands and Africa. Choose the location you are interested in to obtain a "wildlife tour" complete with photographs and narratives on local flora and fauna. This site also has a feature called *Ask the Zookeeper* that allows your students to send e-mail questions to staff members of the zoo.

Brevard Zoo

http://www.brevardzoo.org

Melbourne, Florida's Brevard Zoo features, but is not limited to, animals of Florida and Latin America. You can save time by using the convenient on-site search function. We suggest that you skip the *Internet Zoo View* section of the site because it's primarily a collection of photographs of visitors.

Buffalo Zoological Gardens

http://drew.buffalo.k12.ny.us/drew/tours/zoo/zootours.html

Let the students of the Dr. Charles R. Drew Magnet School (grade 4-8) in Buffalo, New York, take you on a tour of the Buffalo Zoological Gardens. Students and teachers tell you about the American bison, the animals of the Asian forest, bears, predators, primates, rare and nocturnal animals, and reptiles. Some of the animals also have sound samples. The trip is further personalized by brief biographies and photographs of the student writers.

California Living Museum (CALM)

http://bizweb.lightspeed.net/~calm

CALM is a zoo, botanical garden, and natural history museum that displays over 250 unreleasable animals native to California. Your students will be greeted by Caliente the Badger, who will show them the way to the Herpetelogical Center and introduce them to the San Joaquin kit fox, birds of prey, Whiskers the mountain lion, the mule deer, and other denizens. He not only introduces you but also imparts scientific information, such as the animal's genus and species (he himself is known as *taxidea taxus*), descriptions, and information about the animal's natural environment. Younger students will want to visit *Kid's Stuff,* which has activities and games, including downloadable mountain lion and raccoon masks to cut out and color, a coyote picture, and a grizzly color-by-number picture that also involves simple subtraction. If your students e-mail the correct answer to a specific question, such as the difference between antlers and horns, they may win a "surprise."

Cheyenne Mountain Zoo

http://www.cmzoo.org

This Colorado zoo allows you to visit the Asian highlands, wolf woods, and the world of the primate. Of special interest is the live giraffe cam, with a different photograph every three to four minutes, as well as an archive of giraffe cam photos. The Cheyenne Mountain Zoo frequently changes exhibits, so keep checking for new ones.

Cub Den

http://www.nature-net.com/bears/cubden.html

The Den, designed for younger children, is "for bears everywhere and for those children who are on their side." A child can learn that a young bear is able to eat 50 hamburgers and 12 large orders of fries per day. There is also a collection of amazing facts and numerous photographs. Don Middleton, the proprietor, insists that "Bears need each child to believe that they can make a difference in the world."

The Froggy Page

http://frog.simplenet.com/froggy

Sandra Loosemore, a research programmer at Yale, has created *The Froggy Page*, and right from the first sentence, you know you have entered a unique place. "This page contains links to froggy things from various places on the Net for your enjoyment. Ribbet!" By clicking on the word *ribbet*, you will hear an actual frog sound. If that one sound whets your appetite, you can then choose from a menu of other frog sounds: blurp, ka-blurp, East Texas frog croaks, peep-peep, and lots of greedeeps. That is just the beginning of the frog information and resources. There are mythic tales about frogs (including a Native American myth), short stories and poems, frog songs, frog clip art, silly frog images (which include cartoons and a photo of a child with a frog in his mouth), famous frogs (including the Frog Prince and Kermit), and a game of tic-tac-toad. There is also a great deal of serious information about frogs, including a link to a site that allows students to perform a complete on-line frog dissection.

Horses

See Chapter 1— Horse, History of.

The Knoxville Zoo

http://loki.ur.utk.edu/ut2kids/zoo/zoo.html

Kim Widner, a zoology student at the University of Tennessee, has instituted an animal enrichment project at the Knoxville Zoo. Animal enrichment is about constructing activities for animals that keep them active and occupied. Your students can visit the animals at the zoo and see photographs of bears clawing at ice blocks to get at fish frozen inside, tigers stalking and pouncing on balls, and bears pawing at pipes stuffed with honey. Each photograph is accompanied by texts about the animals and how the enrichment activities relate to natural behaviors. The emphasis of this site is on conservation and thoughtful, benevolent care of animals. There is also a glossary of zoological and conservation terms.

Metro Washington Park Zoo

http://www.zooregon.org

This Portland, Oregon, zoo contains extensive exhibits classified by type of animal and geographic environment. Visit the Alaskan tundra, the African rain forest, the Cascades, and other regions. The path *Activities* contains a quiz and pages to color. You can also read about births and obtain information on "101 things you can do to help save animals and their habitats."

National Zoo

http://www.si.edu/natzoo

The National Zoo at the Smithsonian contains an extensive photograph gallery and educational games. The games, found by choosing *Zoo Highlights* and then *Educational Games*, are designed to help educators take advantage of on-site materials and include crossword puzzles, word searches, and a game in which your students can match wits with an orangutan to see who is better at learning symbols that correspond to words. Of special interest is the *Lecture Center,* where you can listen to and watch slide shows presented by Smithsonian personnel. There is also a research-oriented part of the exhibit, where you will find photographs and information on a satellite elephant tracking project in Malaysia, the kimodo dragon, migratory birds, and other projects.

Oakland Zoo

http://www.oaklandzoo.org

This California zoo exhibit is arranged in biomes or alphabetically by animal. The exhibits are in video, print, and audio formats. The path *Cool Stuff* contains animal facts, a quiz, and word games.

Oklahoma City Zoological Park

http://www.cpb.uokhsc.edu/okc/okczoo/zoomap.html

This is the oldest zoo in the Southwest. Visit the butterfly attractant garden (includes a movie), the hoofed animal exhibit, the children's zoo, and other exhibits.

Rat Atlas

http://www.loni.ucla.edu/ratdata/Rat.html

The UCLA Laboratory of Neuro-Imaging has developed a 3-D digital map of rat anatomy. This is a fairly technical site.

Santa Ana Zoo

http://santaanazoo.org/tour

The Santa Ana Zoo in California hosts this site, which takes you on a multimedia tour of the facility. Tour the main zoo, the African aviary, the Amazon exhibit, the Australian yard, the bald eagle exhibit, the rainforest area, the conservation exhibit, the South American Yard, and endangered species. There is also an on-line quiz.

Turtle Trax

http://www.turtles.org

This site is devoted to marine turtles. Exhibits range from photographs to scientific information. There is also a "Turtle Glossary" and a

"Kidz Corner," which has stories, student essays and art, coloring pages, and information on how to build a turtle sundae.

Wilding Heritage Farm

http://www.islandnet.com/~wilding/homepage.html

The Wilding Heritage Farm, located on Vancouver Island in British Columbia, is a conservation center for rare breeds of farm animals. Students can view and learn about animals on the farm, such as the Newfoundland pony, the Oxford down sheep, the Dorset horn, and the karakul.

Wildlife of Nebraska

http://ngp.ngpc.state.ne.us/wildlife/critters.html

Nebraska's sand hill cranes, deer, birds, antelope, beavers, and other wildlife are pictured and profiled. You can also hear the actual sounds of many of the animals.

Wolves

http://www.wolf.org

The award-winning International Wolf Center focuses on educating people about wolves and dispelling myths. They teach that wolves howl at each other—not at the moon—and they "use the language of predators and prey, dominance and submission, play posture, and scent making to make the wolf real." There is an extensive collection of information and wolf images under the heading *Telemetry Data*.

CHAPTER 4

Outer Space

Have you been to outer space recently? Why not take your students to the sun, Jupiter, Mars, outer galaxies, or black holes? The less adventuresome might prefer staying on the ground and viewing outer space through robotic telescopes or visiting virtual observatories. Whatever your choice, such institutions as NASA and Los Alamos National Laboratory will be glad to act as your host!

ARMAGH PLANETARIUM

http://star.arm.ac.uk/planet/planet.html

This United Kingdom planetarium site illustrates the history of space exploration and explains "the mysteries of the night sky." View pictures of nebulae, galaxies, and globular and open clusters taken with the planetarium's telescopes.

BRADFORD ROBOTIC TELESCOPE

http://www.telescope.org/rti

The University of Bradford Department of Industrial Technology has a robotic telescope mounted high on the Pennines in West Yorkshire. Anyone with Internet access can use the telescope to look at anything in the northern night sky. The university simply requires registration (free of charge), at which time you will be issued a user name and password. The less daring can look at pictures previously taken by the telescope, such as those of Comet Hyakutake and lunar eclipses.

CELESTIAL CARTOGRAPHY

http://www.lhl.lib.mo.us/pubserv/hos/stars/welcome.htm

This site explores the history of celestial cartography through 44 star atlases and maps covering the period from 1482 to 1851.

CURIOSITY CLUB

http://nisus.sfusd.k12.ca.us/curiosity_club/bridge1.html

The Curiosity Club at Sunnyside School in San Francisco collaborated with the Center for Extreme Ultraviolet Astrophysics in Berkeley, California, and the San Francisco Unified School District to study the collision of Comet Shoemaker-Levy 9 with Jupiter. Watch a movie of Sunnyside students "traveling" with NASA's EUV Explorer satellite, read the collision progress report, take a tour of Explorer, read about mythology connected with Jupiter and comets, and find out what questions scientists are asking. There is a link to an observatory that brings you to spectacular pictures of Jupiter and the collisions. In addition, there are two glossaries and an astral gallery that has collision-inspired art work created by students.

GALAXIES

http://hou.lbl.gov

Hands-on Universe, a government-sponsored initiative to teach students about space, is ready to take your class to the galaxies. They'll even let your students choose the particular galaxy they would like to visit—simply click on different places of the presented image. Students will learn the different parts of galaxies. They then move on to a quiz that asks questions based upon a galaxy photograph. Student responses are automatically checked and scored.

HENRY BUHL JR. PLANETARIUM AND OBSERVATORY

http://www.csc.clpgh.org/index/planet.html

This Pittsburgh site contains an astronomical calendar where you can find out what's going on in the sky. A glossary is included that explains the events. You can also look at a star map showing the current night sky. Administrators suggest that you print the map and take it outside to match its patterns with those in the sky. Other current charts help you find comets and other astronomical phenomena. There are also photographs and "Ask an Astronomer," where questions are asked and answered via e-mail.

LOS ALAMOS NATIONAL LABORATORY

http://bang.lanl.gov/solarsys

Los Alamos National Laboratory will take your class on an educational tour of the solar system. The site contains images and information about the sun, planets, moon, asteroids, comets, and meteoroids. There are over 200 pages of information and over 950 high-resolution images and animations. Students can travel through space by simply clicking on the planet they would like to visit. There are also extensive databases on planets and stars, as well as materials on the history of space exploration. Site administrators are currently in the process of translating all of the materials into Spanish.

MOUNT WILSON OBSERVATORY

http://www.mtwilson.edu/Services/StarMap

Fill out the on-line form and observatory personnel will construct a personalized star map for you showing the exact positions of stars in your location at any given date and time. The star map is sent directly to your computer.

NATIONAL AERONAUTICS AND SPACE ADMINISTRATION (NASA)

NASA has such an extensive web site that we have chosen to break it down into various sections in order to save you time exploring. Out of all the United States government agencies, NASA is perhaps the one to make the most use of the Internet. It has information for every age level and every level of expertise, with a heavy focus on educating students about space and earth sciences and developing teacher knowledge and expertise. In addition to the materials listed below, NASA's web site also contains lesson plans, teaching resources, grants, scholarships, workshops, and conferences.

http://www.nasa.gov/NASA_homepage.html

NASA's homepage leads to information about the agency's strategic plan, how to become an astronaut, how to see a launch, space exploration, astronomy, and research into the origins of life. There are also on-site videos and sound clips as well as current NASA news.

NASA—Goddard Space Flight Center

http://www.giss.nasa.gov

The NASA Goddard Space Flight Center site contains on-line lessons, information about and pictures of NASA missions, student activities, and curricula materials.

NASA—Jet Propulsion Observatory

http://pds.jpl.nasa.gov/planets

NASA's Jet Propulsion Laboratory has assembled a collection of the best images from the agency's planetary exploration program. There is precise, comprehensive information about the planets and moons in our solar system as well as photographs of and information about the satellites that took and transmitted the images.

NASA On-line Education Center

http://www.nasa.gov/nasa_online_education.html

There are several educational resources at this site, including an *Atlas of Mars*. Other exhibits include an educational game in which students design a subsonic transport, an electronic workbook on various aspects of space flight and solar system exploration, electronic picture books, and more.

NASA—Shuttle Countdown

http://www.ksc.nasa.gov/shuttle/countdown

This site contains detailed information about space shuttle launches, processing, countdowns, and status. Read statistics, shuttle descriptions, and the history of the shuttle program, and learn about the crew and milestones of the program. The site includes both pictures and audio.

NASA—StarChild

http://heasarc.gsfc.nasa.gov/docs/StarChild/StarChild.html

StarChild is NASA's learning center for "young astronomers." Information on the solar system, the universe, and "space stuff" is conveyed through photographs and easy-to-read text. Activities include helping kids to calculate their weight and age on various planets and putting pictures of the various moon phases in order. Although the information is geared toward lower age levels, there is a lot of solid and interesting information for all ages.

NASA—Virtual Observatory

http://skview.gsfc.nasa.gov/easy.html

NASA specifically designed this site for the non-astronomer. Neophytes are able to use this virtual observatory's telescope, which will generate images of any part of the sky using various wave lengths (optical, X-ray, radio, gamma, infrared, and extreme ultraviolet) chosen by the visitor. Your students will be able to view stars, galaxies, nebulae, black holes, neutron stars, supermoon remnants, pulsars and quasars, cosmic rays, interstellar dust, young stars, and white dwarves. We suggest you begin at the orientation page, which will explain how to use the telescope and choose coordinates, projections, brightness, and other parameters.

NASA—Virtual Trips to Black Holes and Neutron Stars

http://antwrp.gsfc.nasa.gov/htmltest/rjn_bht.html

This NASA site contains descriptions and movies that are "scientifically accurate computer animations made with strict adherence to Einstein's Theory of Relativity." The site covers a variety of information geared towards students from "grade to graduate school."

NATIONAL AIR AND SPACE MUSEUM, SMITHSONIAN INSTITUTION

http://www.nasm.si.edu

Simply click on the gallery you choose to visit on the floor plan of this interactive museum—a re-creation of the real thing. Some galleries listed are not available on line. Of particular interest is the *Einstein Planetarium,* where students can learn about the nature of the universe, read about and see the Carl Zeiss Model VIa planetarium instrument (America's first bicentennial gift from the people of West Germany), obtain fact sheets and images of Comet Hyakutaki over Washington, and learn how to receive images from American and Russian polar orbiting satellites using simple equipment. *Exploring the Planets* highlights the history and achievements of planetary exploration.

NINE PLANETS

http://seds.lpl.arizona.edu/nineplanets/nineplanets/nineplanets.html

Bill Arnett, a software programmer and astronomy buff, has compiled this comprehensive site on the planets and major moons of our solar system. The photographs alone are worth the trip, but the amount of information on each celestial body, ranging from technical data to cultural allusions, is equally impressive. There is even animation of such events as orbital paths and space probes, sound excerpts from such sources as Holst's *The Planets*, and links to related information.

NORTHERN LIGHTS PLANETARIUM

http://www.uit.no/npt/nordlyset/nordlyset.en.html

If you want your students to see the Northern Lights, then take them via the Internet to Norway. This exhibit, sponsored by Norway's first public and virtual planetarium, includes articles, descriptions, scientific explanations, pictures, and a movie of the Northern Lights. In case you have difficulty connecting to the above URL, delete the **en**. This will connect you to the Norwegian language version, but the pictures and the movie are beyond language.

ON-LINE ASTRONOMY COURSE

http://www.cnde.iastate.edu/staff/jtroeger/astronomy.html

Jack Troeger, a ninth-grade earth sciences teacher at Ames High School in Ames, Iowa, has put together an Internet astronomy course for middle school and high school students. The course begins with a close-up view of a Dalmatian, and throughout the course, Troeger uses the Dalmatian's spots to explain concepts of the universe. His love of astronomy humanizes the course, such as when he talks about watching shooting stars as a boy growing up in the country. Each section of the course begins with an overview followed by links to other Internet sites that explain the concepts of the lesson in detail. The course covers such topics as light pollution, buying and making your own binoculars and telescopes, how to take pictures of the stars, and the various components of our galaxy.

SOLAR SYSTEM LIVE

http://www.fourmilab.ch/solar/solar.html

This site allows you to view the entire solar system or the inner planets. Controls allow you to set time and date, viewpoint, observing location, and orbital elements to track an asteroid or comet, etc. Click on any title of any control to display a help page. Custom settings can also be requested.

SPACE TELESCOPE SCIENCE INSTITUTE

http://www.stsci.edu

The Space Telescope Science Institute site at Johns Hopkins contains electronic picture books, images, information from or about the Hubble telescope, and movies and animations of astronomical events, such as galaxy formations and Neptune's rotation. Be sure to check out the *Hubble Telescope's Greatest Hits Gallery*—a collection of stunning photos of our galaxy and beyond.

THE SUN

http://www.astro.uva.nl/michielb/sun/kaft.htm

Hop over to the University of Amsterdam and then take a 20-minute trip to the sun to experience flames larger than ten Earths and solar winds so powerful that they reach beyond Pluto. The end of the tour is somewhat disconcerting because it describes the sun's dying process and the eventual destruction of the Earth and the rest of the solar system. This award-winning tour is available in both English and Dutch.

CHAPTER 5

Culture and Sports

From Balinese to New York City theaters, from bluegrass to Bach, from extreme sports to chess—take your students to worldwide cultural and sporting events. Be sure to keep the male students distracted while your female students visit Girl's World!

BALLET

The New York City Ballet

http://www.nycballet.com

The New York City Ballet is the only performing arts institution that trains its own artists, creates its own works, and performs in its own house. Students can visit this famous institution and learn about the history of the ballet and company performances, obtain dancers' biographies and photographs, and learn how to stage a performance. The section titled *Trivia and Other Fun Stuff* includes interviews with some of the stars, interesting questions, and even pages to color. Be sure to take your students to the *Costume Shop,* where they can learn about those who make the costumes, view famous costumes, and meet the staff. If, by chance, there are questions that haven't been answered in this comprehensive site, the staff will gladly accept e-mail questions. Those who consider themselves too macho for the ballet will enjoy the section *Theater Technical Information,* where they will be able to view detailed floor plans and learn all about lighting and sound systems.

CONCERTS AND MUSICAL ADVENTURES

African-American Classical Composer Archives

http://ezinfo.ucs.indiana.edu/~afamarch/home.html

Bring your students to the African-American Classical Composer Archives of Indiana University, where they can read interviews and biographies, see photographs, and listen to music written or performed by African American musicians and composers. This resource will fit into social studies as well as music classes—several of the musicians and composers interviewed have much to say about the African American experience. For example, bassist Simon Estes talks about performing a wide range of music around the world, except in the United States, where he insists he is being blacklisted or typecast only in black musicals, such as *Porgy and Bess*. Judith Anne Still claims that Gershwin stole the tune for, "I Got Rhythm" from her composer father. You can also hear James DePriest speak and then lead the National Symphony Orchestra in selections from Schwanter's *New Morning for the World*, which includes words written by Martin Luther King, Jr. There are also interviews with other African American composers and conductors, a biography of Leontyne Price, and current news about African Americans in classical music.

American School in Japan

http://iris.asij.ac.jp/music/MusicComp.html

The American School in Japan, a K-12 school with students from over 35 countries, invites you to listen to original student musical compositions. The students composed, sequenced, and digitally recorded the works in their classroom in Tokyo. There are on-site instructions on how to listen to the music, as well as available listening software.

The Blue Highway

http://www.thebluehighway.com

Travel the Blue Highway and help your students gain an understanding of the cultural and social context of the blues. An eloquent introduction sets the tone for this journey, which makes stops at famous sites and blues fests in Chicago and St. Louis. Along the way students will be able to visit famous blues singers and hear their performances. A collection of texts and essays explains the roots, attraction, and beauty of the blues, as well as the genre's links to social events.

Bluegrass

See Chapter 12—Watson, Doc.

Classical Music Concert #1

http://sunsite.unc.edu/wm/snd

Perhaps you'll have a better chance of enhancing your students' appreciation of classical music if they can listen to it on the Internet. There are over a dozen compositions to choose from, including Mendelssohn's *Wedding March*, Beethoven's *9th Symphony*, and several Bach sonatas. Watch out for the link to Madonna at the bottom of this site.

Classical Music Concert #2

http://www.dtx.net/~raborn

This site is organized by periods and types of classical music. Select the style of interest (renaissance, baroque, classical, romantic, impressionists, twentieth century, new composers, Christmas, and choral), and then the composer. The MIDI player required to listen to the music may be obtained on site.

Composers in Electronic Residence (CIER)

http://www.edu.yorku.ca/CIERmain.html

CIER is a nonprofit teacher-run electronic community that allows you and your students to form links with experienced composers and with other teachers and students in classrooms around the world. This is essentially an interactive concert site, designed to explore original student music in the classroom. Through an exchange of MIDI music files and comments, schools are able to communicate with professional composers.

Hellenic Civilization

http://www.greekcivil.ariadne-t.gr/default.html

Access the path **Music Server** to hear Greek Lyric Theater and traditional music.

For other information contained in this site, see Chapter 2—Greece—Hellenic Culture and Civilization.

Rock and Roll Hall of Fame

http://www.rockhall.com

Read about the inductees and hear their sound clips. There is also biographical information and sound clips of early genre influences, such as Robert Johnson. This is essentially a commercial site, so supervision will be necessary to steer students away from sales pitches and commercials.

GIRL'S WORLD ON-LINE CLUBHOUSE

http://www.agirlsworld.com

Described as "the space where girls rule the place," this site is conceived as a clubhouse where girls can band together to boost their self-esteem. For example, there are frequently updated profiles of famous girls, such as Michelle Tractenberg (from *Harriet the Spy*), that include tips (such as reminding girls that they can play with their brother's tinker toys or erector sets because there are lots of female architects). The clubhouse has a list of pen pals, art projects, fun facts, and even "tricks" to play on boys. For example, you can bet a boy that you can predict the score of a baseball game before it even starts (zero to zero of course). New members are encouraged to join (free of charge) via the on-site registration form. Site administrators insist that no last names or closely identifying personal information is given out.

LECTURES AND SPEECHES

Michigan State University Vincent Voice Library

http://web.msu.edu/vincent/index.html

The B. Robert Vincent Voice Library houses tapes of speeches, performances, lectures, interviews, and broadcasts by over 50,000 people recorded over a 100-year period. Not all 50,000 tapes are included on-site, but you can choose from several dozen. There are samples from every United States president, from Cleveland to Clinton, including the entire text of Roosevelt's *Day of Infamy* speech, and Nixon's *Farewell.* Other figures with recordings at the site include Amelia Earhart, Florence Nightingale, Isaac Asimov, Anwar Sadat, and Babe Ruth. There is even a recording of Big Ben.

Michigan State Writers Lecture Series

http://hs1.hst.msu.edu/~cal/celeb

Michigan State University has established Internet audio files of 21 writers who have spoken at the university. Show your class pictures and let them hear brief interview excerpts from writers ranging from such popular authors as Terry McMillan to such serious writers as Joyce Carol Oates, Norman Mailer, and poet Maya Angelou. The site administrators have chosen the juiciest sound bites. For example, Arthur Miller talks about his testimony before the House Un-American Activities Committee and answers questions about Marilyn Monroe.

OPERAS AND OPERETTAS

See also Chapter 10—OnLine Opera Library.

Gilbert and Sullivan

http://diamond.idbsu.edu/GaS/GaS.html

The *Gilbert and Sullivan Archive* contains librettos, plot summaries, pictures of original Gilbert and Sullivan stars, song scores, audio files, and articles. There is even Gilbert and Sullivan clip art.

POETRY READINGS

Contemporary and Classical

http://www.theatlantic.com/atlantic/atlweb/poetry/poetpage.htm

Visit the *Atlantic Monthly* magazine and hear poets read their published works. Featured poets have included Robert Pinsky, who reads excerpts from his translation of the *Inferno*. The publishers also share classical and contemporary poetry and essays from the magazine's archives.

PULITZER PRIZE BOARD

http://www.pulitzer.org

This site was produced for the *Columbia Journalism Review* by the Center for New Media at Columbia University. Visit the site to learn the history of the Pulitzer Prize, meet winners from 1917 to the present time, and obtain works and profiles of past and current prize winners. The site enables students to delve more deeply into the Pulitzer winners—samples of current winners' works are included.

SPORTS AND SPORTING EVENTS

Baseball

See Chapter 1—African American History—Negro Baseball League *and* Negro Leagues Baseball Online Archive.

Bullfighting

http://www.personal.isat.com/bullfights/index2.html

Bullfighting is considered gruesome and inhumane by some and an art form by others. This site takes the latter view while teaching the sport and introducing some of the more famous matadors. There are also statistics and photographs from current bullfights.

Chess

http://caissa.onenet.net/chess

The *Internet Chess Library* contains a collection of chess memorabilia, game data bases, works of art (including boards and pieces), and ratings of both current and inactive chess players. (Just to prove that chess is a cutthroat game, the 100 worst players are also named.)

Dog Sledding

http://www.sleddog.org

The Alaska Dog Mushers' Association will teach you all about the sport of dog sledding. There arc cven tips for your first race (don't forget your snow hook and sled bag).

http://alaska.alaskan.com/~iditarod

In 1925 Nome, Alaska, was threatened by a diphtheria epidemic. The nearest serum was 674 miles away. Twenty dog sledding teams made the trip in 1,275 hours and saved the city of Nome. This event is commemorated in the annual Iditarod race, which begins in Anchorage each year on the first Saturday in March. Modern Iditarod racers now make the 1,200-mile trip in 10 to 12 days. Why not take your students to the next race? You can send away for a teaching packet (details are on site), but even without the packet, your students may participate in "the last great race on Earth." Iditarod participants will show students how to read maps and teach them the official rules, which cover both sportsmanship and care for the dogs and the environment. Some may prefer to hear about the race from the point of view of Zuma the sled dog, who will also gladly accept e-mail. If you're not too tired after the race, you may want to hang around Nome for a while and attend a reindeer potluck dinner and see some of the local sites.

Extreme Sports

See Chapter 10—Get Lost Adventure Magazine.

Gymnastics

http://gymn.digiweb.com/gymn/index.html

Visit the Gymn Forum and meet gymnasts from around the world. They'll tell you all about themselves and the world of gymnastics. You can even take an on-line gymnastics trivia quiz.

Iditarod

See Sports and Sporting Events—Dog Sledding, *above*.

Jump Rope Federation

http://www.usajrf.org

The United States Jump Rope Federation will show and explain how to do some of the advanced level tricks performed by its members at performances and competitions. You can also visit the Alvin Jumperoos and Pure Energy and see how to do the three-person Chinese Wheel.

Lawn Bowling

See Chapter 2—United States—New York—Central Park.

National Basketball Association

http://www.nba.com

Visit the N.B.A. and meet some of the players and coaches, learn the rules of league play and officiating, and obtain schedules, game results, and news about the league.

Scuba Diving

See Chapter 3—Aquatic and Marine Life—Scuba Diving in Maui.

Sports Illustrated for Kids

See Chapter 10—Sports Illustrated for Kids.

White Water Rafting—Running the Nile

See Chapter 2—Nile River.

TELEVISION SHOWS

Street Cents

http://www.halifax.cbc.ca/streetcents

This site is the on-line companion to the award-winning Canadian Broadcast Company's television series. Each week a new topic is covered and added to the archives of the site. Most of the topics are devoted to consumer awareness, such as "Food Safety" (check out instant pudding and what you should know when a health inspector comes to dinner). Students can also see how the show is made.

THEATER

Balinese Shadow Theater

http://www.balibeyond.com/gamelan/shadowinfo.html

Balinese Shadow Play or "wayang kulit" (lit leather figures) is a combination of Indonesian and Indian ritual, lesson, and entertainment in which mythic tales are performed by shadows of hand puppets that are projected onto a screen. Visit this site to learn about the history of shadow theater, primary mythical figures, and Balinese instruments and music. There are also instructions on how to make the puppets and the required screen.

The Glass Menagerie

http://www.susqu.edu/ac_depts/arts_sci/english/lharris/CLASS/WILLIAMS/table.htm

This site is largely devoted to Tennessee Williams's play *The Glass Menagerie*. In addition to biographic materials, students can obtain a plot summary, character sketches, literary criticism, pictures, music, and the entire script of the climactic Scene VII, complete with a footnoted glossary. An on-line video of the scene is also available.

For other information contained in this site, see Chapter 12—Williams, Tennessee.

Kabuki Theater

http://www.fix.co.jp/kabuki/kabuki.html

Ichimura Manjiro, a Japanese actor, has set up this site to explain and honor Kabuki theater. Students can read about the history of Kabuki theater, see video performances, and watch the step-by-step application of traditional make-up. Texts are also available in Japanese.

Les Miserables

http://www.ot.com/lesmis/nov/home.html

If you can't afford tickets, this is the next best option. This site contains a story summary of the musical as well as a complete libretto, photographs, and sound clips. There are also links to the complete Victor Hugo novel. The on-site Hugo biography is every bit as stirring as the novel. If you think it will help, tell your students this is the guy who wrote *The Hunchback of Notre Dame*.

Miss Saigon

http://www.clark.net/pub/rsjdfg

Thanks to a pediatrician at the University of Maryland who is a *Miss Saigon* fan, your class can see scenes from the musical, meet the actors and actresses, obtain the complete libretto, and see and hear video and audio clips. There is also a study guide that deals with such topics as culture and conflict, the Bui Doi, and the Vietnam War. Of special interest is the section covering the creation of a musical through the study of the work of composers, set designers, lighting designers, critics, and actors.

Phantom of the Opera

http://phantom.skywalk.com

Attend the *Phantom of the Opera* without leaving the classroom. There are pictures and a detailed history of the Paris Opera House, a biography of Gaston Leroux, a story summary, sound clips, and images of the performance.

Puppet Theater—Stage Hand Puppets

http://fox.nstn.ca/~puppets/activity.html

The goal of *Stage Hand Puppets*, a Canadian group, is to make children around the world excited about puppets and plays. Children are encouraged to write, design, and direct their own puppet plays. On-site instructions tell children how they can submit their plays, and *Stage Hand Puppets* promises that, if the content is not offensive or inappropriate, they will post the play on their virtual puppet theater. Students can read plays submitted by others. They can also design their own puppets on screen by choosing preformatted facial and body features. Information is also provided on hand shadows and finger, string, and origami puppets.

CHAPTER 6

Art Museums and Galleries

Now you can sit back and enjoy the world's greatest works of art with your students without worrying about keeping order and hushed reverence. The art museums and galleries around the world will open their doors to you. See national and international masterpieces and the works of local artists and artisans. Remember that museums and galleries often change exhibits, so if you don't find exactly what you're looking for in our descriptions, you may still wish to check these sites for possibilities.

AFRICAN ART

See also Detroit Institute of the Arts, *below, and* Houston Museum of Fine Arts, *below*.

Akan and Yoruba Art

http://www.fa.indiana.edu/~conner/africart/home.html

First presented at Peoria's Lakeview Museum of Art and Science, this on-line exhibit presents Yoruba and Akan art in wood and metal. Included in the exhibit is a history of the people of the area, development of the craft, and pictures of the artifacts.

Bayly Museum

http://www.lib.virginia.edu/dic/exhib/93.ray.aa/African.html

The Bayly Museum at the University of Virginia maintains an on-site collection of masks, headdresses, statuettes, and sculpture. Extensive narratives discuss the objects in terms of form, composition, meaning, and their relationship to various African societies.

ALAMKARA: 5,000 YEARS OF INDIAN ART

See Chapter 2—India.

ANDY WARHOL MUSEUM

http://www.warhol.org/warhol/warhol.html

Take your students on a floor-by-floor tour of the Warhol Museum in Pittsburgh. Although there is not a lot of information at this site, what there is, like Warhol, is fascinating. There are brief texts on his magazine, *Interview* (he admits that he started the publication to get free tickets to premieres), as well as a sample inventory of one of his several hundred time capsules. (Warhol is described as "an obsessive saver who never threw anything out.")

ARTE MAYA TZ' UTUHIC MUSEUM

See Chapter 2—Guatemala.

BRITISH ART AND THE ORIGINS OF MODERN CHILDHOOD

See Chapter 8—British Art and the Origins of Modern Childhood.

CARIBBEAN ART GALLERY

http://www.oir.ucf.edu/bryant

The Caribbean Art Gallery was developed by the Bryant Foundation at the University of Central Florida. The exhibit includes a collection of art organized by Antigua, Aruba, Barbados, the Cayman Islands, Curacao, Florida, Grenada, Guyana, Haiti, Jamaica, Martinique, Puerto Rico, and the Virgin Islands.

CEZANNE, PAUL

See Monet, Claude, *below*.

CHESLEY BONESTELL ART GALLERY

http://www.secapl.com/bonestell/Top.html

Chesley Bonestell was originally an architect who worked on major structures, including the Golden Gate Bridge. At the age of 50, he began a second career as a motion picture special effects artist and worked on such famous movies as *The War of the Worlds*. This led to his third career as an artist. Bonestell is well known for his conceptions of outer space long before the era of space exploration. Meet the artist and tour the Bonestell gallery, where some of his most famous paintings are on display.

DALI, SALVADORE

http://www.empower.net/dali/dalimain.html

Students can view the art work of Salvadore Dali and read explanations and analyses of his work.

For other information contained in this site, see Chapter 12—Dali, Salvadore.

DALLAS MUSEUM OF ART

http://www.unt.edu/dfw/dma/www/dma.htm or
gopher://gopher.unt.edu
Path: Denton, Dallas & Fort Worth Information & Resources/Dallas Museum of Art—Information and Images

The Dallas Museum of Art has a repository of paintings, multimedia brochures, and electronic teaching packets. There are a variety of topics covered, including the deities of ancient Peru, Eskimo spirit masks, furniture crafted for Spanish colonists and Anglo-American merchants, and art from the Pilgrims, pioneers, clerics, soldiers, and slaves. The teaching packets include background texts and activities that tie in to the images.

DETROIT INSTITUTE OF THE ARTS

http://www.dia.org/index2.html

On-line exhibitions include Ancient Art, which takes you on a tour of the ancient Mediterranean world of Egypt, Greece, Rome, and Islam. Works range from prehistoric objects from the caves of Mount Carmel in Israel to gold artifacts from the Bronze Age in Ireland. Every artistic medium is represented, including pottery, stone, glass, textiles, and metal. Works include sculpture, paintings, weapons, armor, jewelry, textiles, and mummies. There is also an exhibition of tapestries that includes 20 master works from the late fifteenth to the early twentieth century representing nearly all major European weaving centers and tapestries from 1500 on: Renaissance tapestries from the leading sixteenth-century weaving centers of Brussels and Burges, seventeenth-century hangings made at the French Beauvais and royal Gobelins factories, and one of the most important English arts and crafts tapestries in the United States—The Passing of Venus. Texts identify the allegorical, Biblical, historical, and literary themes of each of the works, as well as artistic styles, uses, etc. The *African Form and Imagery Gallery* has more than 70 objects arranged according to function.

DIEGO RIVERA MUSEUM

http://www.diegorivera.com/diego_home_eng.html

This exhibit is available in both English and Spanish. It examines and shows the works of Diego Rivera (1886-1957), the muralist painter from Mexico. The virtual museum contains a small collection of his paintings and murals. Although there is little explication about his art, the biographical material is extremely detailed.

ELECTRONIC ART

http://www.sysnet.it/~lpacciar/indexuk.html

Anchise Pucchi, an 85-year-old Italian artist, has proven that one is never too old to learn. Pucchi has spent a lifetime painting, sculpting, and engraving, and has turned his considerable talents to electronic art. See his "paintings," meet the artist, and learn about the art of electronic painting at this site.

ESCHER, M. C.

http://lonestar.texas.net/~escher

Students love the strange optical illusions of M. C. Escher's works, and this site leads you to several of them. There is also a collection of Escher quotes and anecdotes, many of which are as strange as his works, and an Escher forum where your students are free to post their own opinions of Escher's works and read what others have said.

FRACTAL ART

See Chapter 7—Fractal Art.

FREDERICK R. WEISMAN ART MUSEUM

http://hudson.acad.umn.edu

The Frederick R. Weisman Art Museum is located at the Minneapolis campus of the University of Minnesota. The museum holds a permanent collection of over 13,000 objects, a selection of which are contained at this site. Featured artists include Marsden Hartley, Alfred Maurer, and Georgia O'Keefe, but there are also individual works by a dozen other artists.

GLENBOW

http://www.glenbow.org

Glenbow is Canada's foremost center of history and art, housing a museum of western heritage, international cultural collections, an art gallery, a library, and archives of western Canadian history. The art gallery has a collection of oil paintings, watercolors, prints, drawings, photographs, sculptures, and contemporary works of various media. Focusing on western Canada, the collection covers the spectrum from the nineteenth century.

See also Chapter 8—Glenbow.

HELLENIC CIVILIZATION

http://www.greekcivil.ariadne-t.gr/default.html

Almost every art museum and gallery in Greece is accessible via this site. There is a list of museums, each of which has an introductory section with an excellent description of available on-site materials. Virtually every period and medium is covered, including images of important and historically significant architectural features of several of the museum buildings. In addition to what one might expect on the tour, there are some specialty museums, such as The Cartoon Museum, which displays caricatures and comic strips by Greek artists; the Ilial Lalaounis Jewelry Museum; the Philatelic Museum, with exhibits of post boxes, safes, postal stamping machines, bags and horns used by postmen, and other articles of the postal, telegraph, and telephone services; and the Teriade Museum Library. Teriade (1889-1983) was a publisher who cooperated with leading twentieth-century artists to produce the so-called Great Books. There are examples of illustrations by Matisse, Picasso, and Chagall.

For other information contained in this site, see Chapter 2—Greece.

HOUSTON MUSEUM OF FINE ARTS

http://mfah.org

The Museum of Fine Arts in Houston, Texas, has an extensive exhibit depicting the art of world cultures from antiquity to the present, including African sculpture, American paintings, ancient art, decorative art, impressionist painting, twentieth-century sculpture, landscaped gardens, and decorative art. None of these areas are heavily represented—this site is intended to be a sampling of the museum's holdings—but the texts are clear, and the few chosen examples in each area are striking.

INTERNATIONAL MUSEUM OF THE HORSE

http://www.imh.org

The museum's Equestrial Art Gallery displays photographs by Charles Rumph and bronze horses by Edwin Bogucki.

See also Chapter 1—Horse, History of.

KRANNERT ART MUSEUM—UNIVERSITY OF ILLINOIS

http://www.art.uiuc.edu/kam/Misc

The Krannert Art Museum at the University of Illinois in Champaign-Urbana features a permanent on-line display of pre-Columbian, Asian, and African art, as well as an American and European collection that spans the fifteenth through twentieth centuries. In addition to the permanent displays, there are frequently changing temporary exhibitions, not only of art, but also of such topics as how curators, conservators, art historians, and scientists work together to preserve, interpret, and deduce historical information from ancient art objects.

LEONARDO DA VINCI MUSEUM

See Chapter 12—da Vinci, Leonardo.

LOS ANGELES COUNTY ART MUSEUM

http://www.lacma.org/Exhibits/default.htm

This site contains past and present exhibitions from the Los Angeles County Art Museum that cover such areas as American art, ancient and Islamic art, costumes and textiles, decorative arts, European paintings and sculpture, Far Eastern art, Indian and southeastern art, photographs, prints and drawings, and twentieth-century art. The main exhibitions lean toward the unusual, such as an exhibition of German Expressionists' renditions of Old Testament art.

MONET, CLAUDE

http://www.ugrad.cs.jhu.edu/~baker/monet.html

Brad Baker, at Johns Hopkins University, wants to show your class dozens of Monet's paintings. He's such a Monet devotee, that he even has some Monet wallpaper for your computer screen you can download for free. Baker also includes biographic and critical information about the French Impressionist and provides links to other Monet resources as well as to Cezanne and Van Gogh sites.

MUSEUM OF MODERN ART (MOMA)

http://www.moma.org/webprojects.html

New York City's MOMA's web site is hosted by The School of Visual Arts. The site is representative of some of the museum's collections, with a focus on architecture, materials design, video, and sculpture. Exhibits change regularly.

MUSEUM OF SINGAPORE ART AND HISTORY

See Chapter 2—Singapore.

NATIONAL MUSEUM OF AMERICAN ART

http://www.nmaa.si.edu

The Smithsonian Institution's Museum of American Art houses an extensive collection of crafts, sculptures, paintings, and other works of art. The *White House Collection of Crafts* has an introduction (audio) by Hillary Rodham Clinton. You can choose the medium of interest (ceramics, glass, metal, or wood) or take a guided tour. The site includes text, photographs, graphics, video, and audio. Exhibits include, but are not limited to, "William H. Johnson," "Paul Manship," "Land and Landscape—Views of America's Past and Present," and "Pueblo Indian Watercolors." There are also works by over a dozen artists, filed alphabetically by artist, title, and category. Exhibits include "Between Home and Heaven: Contemporary Landscape Photographs," "Women Artists," and "Hispanic American Art."

NATIONAL PALACE MUSEUM—TAIWAN

See Chapter 2—Taiwan.

NATIVE AMERICAN ART

See also National Museum of American Art, *above*.

American Indian Network—Great Lakes Region

http://glrain.cic.net/dia

The Great Lakes Region American Indian Network site examines Native American art from the North American woodlands and plains between 1780 and 1920. Included are clothing and bags made from porcupine quills, woven sashes, jewelry, and smoking pipes. The exhibit is a collaboration between the Detroit Institute of Arts and David Penney, curator of the Native American Art Museum.

Institute of American Indian Arts

http://www.artnatam.com

Your students can learn civics, history, and art when they visit the Institute of American Indian Arts. The works of five Native American artists from the Cheyenne, Shoshone, Creek, Pima, and Comanche tribes are on display. Artists are chosen by a juried process, and works are searchable by either artist or subject matter (animal, contemporary style, traditional style, dancer, landscape, lore and teaching, tribal journey, spirit, etc.). Also included are the biographies and e-mail addresses of each artist.

Inter-Tribal Gallery

http://www.indart.com/gallery/gallery.htm

The Inter-Tribal Gallery contains a collection of paintings, sculpture, pottery, cultural items, beadwork, kachinas, and other works of art, primarily encompassing Native American tribes and artists from the southwest. In addition to the varied and numerous works of fine and decorative art, there are links to web resources for individual Indian tribes.

Northwest Coast Tribal Art

http://orca.inuitart.com/nwcoast/nwart.html

This site contains a collection of Northwest Coast Tribal art covering a variety of artists from British Columbia. Both traditional and contemporary works are featured, including totem poles, masks, jewelry, and prints.

Powersource Gallery

http://www.powersource.com/powersource/gallery/default.html

Powersource Gallery is a collection of Native American artistic symbols portraying "powerful people, powerful places, and powerful objects." In addition to works of art, there are texts on powerful places in Texas, New Mexico, and Arizona, and sections on ceremonial dances, powerful people, and powerful women. The *Powerful People* section includes such historical figures as Cochise, Geronimo, and Sitting Bull (as well as lesser known Native Americans, in case you wish to expand your students' knowledge beyond the usual celebrities), and such contemporary figures as Ben Nighthorse Campbell, the Colorado senator. Students may submit their own nominations by e-mail. Powerful Native American women are included in the *Women Spirit* section, and, yes, Pocahontas is included, in case your students are interested in learning the true story. (According to the site, Wayne Newton, part Cherokee, is negotiating with England for the return of Pocahontas's remains.)

Sisochi Gallery

http://www.yosemitegold.com/nativeamerican

Your students may enjoy touring the Sisochi Gallery, located near Yosemite National Park. There are separate exhibits on northwest coast ceremonial masks and carvings, California baskets, Navajo war axes, drums, and rattles, and North American pottery, as well as works of art by contemporary Native American artisans. After your students are through touring the gallery, they may wish to go on a tour of Yosemite and the surrounding gold country, where they may view pictures and maps and learn local history.

PEABODY ESSEX MUSEUM OF ART

http://www.pem.org

The Peabody Essex Museum of Art in Salem, Massachusetts frequently changes exhibitions, but you can always count on something with a uniquely American theme. When we last checked, there were exhibits of early American architecture and furniture. There are usually international exhibits as well, with an emphasis on decorative objects and sculpture. Peabody Essex also lists education resources for teachers with occasional free material. During the release of the movie *The Crucible,* middle and high school teachers could send away for a curriculum guide for teaching about the Salem witchcraft trials. You might also check here if you're teaching about anything with a maritime theme. The tables of contents, with a sample article from the museum's quarterly magazine, *The American Neptune,* a journal of maritime history and arts, are available on site.

PHOTOGRAPHY AND PHOTOJOURNALISM

See also Chapter 10—Photojournalism *and* Life Magazine.

California Museum of Photography

http://cmp1.ucr.edu

The California Museum of Photography at the University of California-Riverside has extensive on-line photographic exhibits, including "Los Angeles 1905-1930," "San Francisco 1900-1910," "California Industry," "Pasadena 1890's," "Logging and Lumbering 1895-1905," "Trains," "Ellis Island," "Russia Before the Revolution," "Japan ca. 1880," and "Shirley Temple." Students can also visit the *Virtual Magnifying Glass,* where images are mapped to reveal details. There are lesson plans and activities that emphasize sight, motion, time, and space. Activities include building a thaumatrope (an optical toy), making flipboard movies, and constructing a zoetrope motion device. There are also photographs from Graceland and a section on contemporary German photography. Students should be supervised when navigating this site because teachers may consider some materials inappropriate, such as an exhibit of guns, and photographs by Robert Mapplethorpe. These appear under the heading *Previous Exhibits.*

The Daguerrian Society

http://www.austinc.edu/dag/home.html

The Daguerrian Society, founded in 1988 is an organization of individuals and institutions with an interest in the art, history, and practice of the daguerreotype photographic process. While browsing through the exhibit, you might want to download the music to Robert Schuman's *Traumerei,* provided on site. The society provides several on-line galleries that display examples of daguerreotype centered on various themes. These include *Daguerreotypes in the Open* (an effort to document the changing face of a nation), *Reflections of an Era*, *The Portraits*, and *Modern Daguerreotypes*. Other information includes a history of the daguerreotype, an illustrated step-by-step description of the process, and nineteenth- and twentieth-century texts.

Edgerton Center On-Line Photo Gallery

http://the-tech.mit.edu/Gallery/gallery.html

The Edgerton Gallery at the Massachusetts Institute of Technology exhibits students' latest work in high-speed photography and videography.

George Eastman House: International Museum of Photography and Film

http://www.eastman.org

The George Eastman House is located on historic East Avenue in Rochester, New York. The 12½-acre museum, Eastman's former urban estate, houses an extensive collection of photography that focuses on such themes as the history of photographic albums, immigration to America, a comprehensive examination of Clarence White's career, a study of the work of Betty Han, and Indonesian film posters. You can also tour Eastman's mansions and gardens.

For further information contained in this site, see Chapter 12—Eastman, George.

Library of Congress American Memory Exhibit

http://lcweb.loc.gov/homepage/lchp.html

Choose the path **American Memory / Prints and Photos** to access a number of samples from actual exhibits contained within the Library of Congress. These include "Carl Van Vechten Photographs, 1932-1964" (portraits of celebrities, including many from the Harlem Renaissance), "Color Photographs from the Farm Security Administration and Office of War Info, Ca. 1938-1944" (photographs of rural and small town America and scenes of the war mobilization effort), "Daguerreotypes, 1942-1962" (includes images and a detailed exhibition of how the photographs are preserved), "Evolution of the Conservation Movement, 1850-1920," "Gottscho-Schleisner Photographs, 1935-1955," "Selected Civil War Photographs," and "World Transportation Commission Photographs, 1894-1896."

For other information on this site, see Chapter 1—Library of Congress—American Memory.

Photo Perspectives

http://www.i3tele.com/photoperspectives/museum/html/perspectives.html

This award-winning site presents photographic essays with accompanying texts of contemporary and past subjects. Features have included pieces on endangered wildlife, Sarajevo, the American Ballet Theater, and others.

Photojournalistic Essays

See Chapter 10—Photojournalism.

Secrets of the Dark Chamber: The Art of the American Daguerreotype

http://www.nmaa.si.edu/secrets/secretshtml/secrets.html

The Smithsonian Institution's National Museum of Modern Art site features rarely seen examples of early daguerreotypes from private and public collections. Students can also obtain a history of the daguerreotype and meet the exhibit's curator. An audio tour is also available.

Stereographs

http://192.253.114.31/Projects

The students at Patch American High School in Stuttgart, Germany, have put together an old-fashioned stereoscopic exhibit of Yosemite National Park, so that you can simultaneously teach your students about the old stereoscopic viewers and show them primitive 3-D black-and-white photos of Yosemite. This is part of an ongoing project in which students are investigating how to make random dot stereograms using modern computer software. Stereographs—photographs that recreate the sensation of 3-D viewing when viewed through a stereoscope—were popular during the nineteenth and early twentieth centuries. Students can also learn about the history of stereoscopes and see pictures of actual viewers.

For other information contained in this site, see Chapter 11—Schools—Germany—Patch American High School—Stuttgart, Germany.

POSTCARDS

Postcard Gallery

http://www.xe.net/postcard

The Postcard Gallery collects postcards from all over the world. You can select the *Cool Postcard of the Month* or any of the exhibits from the site's extensive archives.

The Postcard Shop

http://postcards.www.media.mit.edu/Postcards

At the Electronic Postcard Shop, students can customize their own virtual postcard by selecting artwork, typing in a message, and then e-mailing the card. The available artwork includes several famous paintings and photographs.

PUSHKIN MUSEUM OF FINE ARTS

http://www.RoSprint.net/art/museum/pushkin

The Pushkin Museum of Fine Arts in Moscow, which holds one of the major art collections in Russia, features foreign works of art from ancient times to the present. Included in the exhibit is ancient Egyptian art acquired from the Russian Egyptologist Vladimir Golenischev; art from the fourth-century B.C. Greek late classical period; seventeenth-century Flemish, Dutch, and Spanish paintings; seventeenth- and eighteenth-century Italian art and sculpture; and seventeenth- to twentieth-century French art. Although the collection is wide ranging and impressive, there is practically no accompanying text, so supplementary materials are needed.

RENAISSANCE AND BAROQUE ARCHITECTURE

http://www.lib.virginia.edu/dic/collections/collections.html

Browse through the collection of more than 500 images organized under approximately 25 categories. The images were scanned from slides taken by Professor C. W. Westfall, University of Virginia, School of Architecture, Department of Architectural History.

THE ROSSETTI ARCHIVE

http://jefferson.village.virginia.edu/rossetti/rossetti.html

Thanks to the University of Virginia, your students are able to visit an exhibit of the complete works of Dante Gabriel Rossetti (1828-1882), the pre-Raphaelite poet and painter. There are images of his manuscripts, early printed texts and proofs, drawings, and paintings. You may even take your students directly inside Rossetti's studio, which is so detailed that there are sketches pinned on the walls. Special software required for the studio visit is available on site.

SAN FRANCISCO FINE ARTS MUSEUM

http://www.thinker.org

This may well be the most ambitious fine arts project on the Internet. Over 60,000 images of paintings and sculptures are currently available, with more in the works. In order to protect artists' copyrights, works are presented in a digitalized format that provides excellent quality on screen, but poor quality when printed. With 60,000 images, it's a safe bet that whatever you're searching for is here. The on-site search function makes the site easily manageable.

SONOMA STATE UNIVERSITY ART GALLERY

http://www.sonoma.edu/ArtGallery/exhibits.html

The Sonoma State University Art Gallery is one of the largest art institutions in the North Bay region devoted to changing exhibits of modern and contemporary art. There are many on-line exhibitions at this site, some of which you may want to monitor. Exhibits range from the works of contemporary New York artists (hence, the potential need for supervision) to "Waura: Drawings of the Waura Indians," an exhibit which grew out of the research of Dr. Vera Penteado Coelho, an anthropologist living in Brazil. The exhibit features drawings by the Wauras, an isolated tribe living in the Amazon region. The drawings depict images from Waura culture and mythology, as well as motifs found in their intricate body decorations. There is also an on-line lesson plan that encourages students to learn the difference between works of art and people who make them in various times and places. The lesson plans, which make connections between art, anthropology, and geography, can be adapted to any grade level.

TOKUGAWA ART MUSEUM

See Chapter 2—Japan.

WEB MUSEUM

http://sunsite.unc.edu/wm/paint

This is the site of the Web Museum, a collaboration with the University of North Carolina. There are works by and biographies of hundreds of artists, from Paul Cezanne to Lewis Carroll. You can choose what you want to learn about by topic or by artist. There is also an on-site glossary. Over 200,000 people per week connect to the site to view the images and learn about pre-Renaissance Gothic through twentieth-century art.

WORLD ART TREASURES

http://sgwww.epfl.ch/BERGER/index.html

With so much to learn and so little time, you might want to consider a field trip that combines art and history lessons. Friends of Jacques-Edouard Berger—late curator of the Museum of Fine Arts in Lausanne, Switzerland, worldwide traveler, and art collector—have honored him by setting up the Jacques-Edouard Berger Foundation, which sponsors this site. It interweaves a collection of great world art with Berger's own words and with texts that attempt to place viewers back in time, as if they were experiencing the art when it was new. There are six exhibits, with more planned. "Pilgrimage to Abydos" takes you to ancient Egypt, while "Roman Portraits from Egypt" covers Egyptian art from a slightly later period. There are also exhibits on Vermeer and Botticelli, and a stunning exhibition of Renaissance Gardens. The exhibit *Shared Vision* covers several of the voyages that Berger made. There is also an exhibit that covers the art of southeast Asia, China, Japan, and India.

CHAPTER 7

Mathematics and Logic

Now you can cover the history of mathematics and logic from Aristotle and the abacus to computer-generated fractal art. Welcome to optical illusions, mind-games, and the latest methods for teaching math from some of the leading mathematicians and educational theorists. Let your students ask questions of the experts in mathematics and logic and match wits with students around the world.

THE CALCULATOR MUSEUM

http://www.teleport.com/~dgh/hpmuseum.html

Dave Hicks, who works for Intel, invites you to visit his Hewlett-Packard Calculator Museum (which is not affiliated with the corporation of the same name). In an act of hubris, the history of calculators is divided into two periods—from 1614-1968 (or pre-Hewlett-Packard), and from 1968 on. Your students will probably be more interested in the first period, which features slide rules, really primitive contraptions, and bulky adding machines from the 1940s and 1950s.

CALCULUS GRAPHICS GALLERY

http://www.math.psu.edu/dna/graphics.html

Take your students to the technology classroom at Pennsylvania State University to see this collection of graphical demonstrations developed for first-year calculus students. Through the use of images, computer animation, on-line worksheets, and other resources, students will learn to compute the volume of water in a tipped glass, to understand and predict how a ball bounces, and to figure out other basic calculus problems.

COMPUTERS AND OFFICE AUTOMATION

http://granite.sentex.net/~ccmuseum

Do you remember the days of keypunch operators and sorting machines? Your students will find it hard to believe that it used to take an entire room of mainframe computers to do the work of the PC that now sits on a desk. The *Computerseum* is dedicated to preserving the history of data processing and office automation through photographs and texts. Administrators of this site are proud to announce that *Globe and Mail* refers to the exhibit as "Canada's Geek Museum."

CURVES, FAMOUS

http://www-groups.dcs.st-and.ac.uk/~history/Curves/Curves.html

St. Andrew University in Scotland has accumulated data on over 50 curves. Click on any item in the index to see the curve's equation, history, and some of its associated curves. There are a variety of choices, from "Asteroid" to "Watts," the curve named after the inventor of the steam engine.

FRACTAL ART

ArtByMath Gallery

http://www.ArtByMath.com

The ArtByMath Gallery presents fractal art from Cyberlight Matrix. Although the site is largely a commercial for the company's products, students can visit the on-line gallery and see fractal images of celestial landscapes, fractal life-forms, and celestial creatures. This site also has an extensive list of links to other fractal art galleries.

For an explanation of fractal art, see Fractal Art—The Fractal Microscope, *below.*

Don Archer's Fractal Art Gallery

http://www.ingress.com/~arch/index.html

Don Archer's Fractal Art Gallery has dozens of vivid images of his work, including fractal zoos (both real and imaginary), cameras, gardens, and fault lines. Mr. Archer's prints have been exhibited in several shows in New York City, and his work is included in the collection of the Ball State University Art Museum in Muncie, Indiana. An interesting feature of this site is the "U-Draw Fractal," where Mr. Archer will create a fractal from random numbers and functions provided by your students. The results will appear on site. Even those who don't understand the concept will enjoy the artwork.

For an explanation of fractal art, see Fractal Art—The Fractal Microscope, *below.*

Fractal Gallery

http://sprott.physics.wisc.edu/carlson.htm

Carlson's Fractal Gallery has dozens of images with explanations and the formulas from which they were created. If you can understand the explanations, then you probably already know what fractal art is. If you can't understand, just relax and enjoy the art or see the next listing.

The Fractal Microscope

http://www.ncsa.uiuc.edu/Edu/Fractal

The Fractal Microscope is an interactive tool designed by the Education Group at the National Center for Supercomputing Applications for the exploration of the Mandlebrot set and other fractal patterns. The on-site fractal art display is accompanied by explanations of how to use fractal art in the K-12 classroom. Such topics as scientific notation, the coordinates of systems and graphing, number systems, convergence, and divergence are covered. In their words, "Fractal geometry mixes art with mathematics to demonstrate that equations are more than just a collection of numbers. Using fractal geometry, students can visually model much of what they see in nature, such as coastlines and mountains."

Fractal Movie Archive

http://www.cnam.fr/fractals/anim.html

Students can travel to France to visit a fractal animation gallery. Texts explaining the construction of the exhibit are included in both French and English.

Interactive Fractal Art

http://reality.sgi.com/employees/rck/hydra/gallery/index1.html

There are a total of 1,700 fractal images in this gallery, most of which can be manipulated in order to allow exploration of various fractal positions. Options include zooming in or out, or two- and three-dimensional views.

GEOMETRY CENTER

http://www.geom.umn.edu

The Geometry Center is a joint collaboration between the National Science Foundation and the Technology Center at the University of Minnesota, a partnership that has succeeded in making this area of study interesting, practical, and easy to understand. Students will be interested in the *Interactive Geometry Gallery,* in which they are able to participate in many hands-on activities. For example, the *Web Pisces* allows the implicit computation of defined curves on a plane and the *Build a Rainbow Gallery* answers common questions about this natural phenomenon by examining a mathematical model of light passing through a water droplet. This is a small sample of the available activities. There is also free software and other data.

THE GREY LABYRINTH—A PLAYGROUND FOR THE CURIOUS MIND

http://www.wx3.com/labyrinth/index.htm

Visit the Grey Labyrinth and test your wits against the three wisest sages. See if you can choose the best solution from the choices faced by the accountant, and access numerous other brain teasers. For upper grade levels—most of the problems require complex reasoning.

HISTORY OF MATHEMATICS

See also Chapter 9—Science—Museums—History—Renaissance Science.

http://www.mhs.ox.ac.uk/exhibits/index.htm

The Museum of the History of Science at Oxford concentrates on practical mathematics and geometry. *The Geometry of War, 1500-1750,* concentrates on Renaissance mathematicians who applied geometry to practical disciplines, such as navigation, surveying, cartography, gunnery, and range finding. The exhibit *The Measurers: A Flemish Image of Mathematics in the Sixteenth Century* deals with the practical mathematics movement of Renaissance Europe.

LOS ALAMOS NATIONAL LABORATORY'S MEGA MATH

http://www.c3.lanl.gov:80/mega-math

The intention of this site is to bring unusual and important math ideas and concepts to schools. Several areas of mathematics are covered, and each section includes activities, vocabulary, background information, ideas, and key concepts. *The Most Colorful Math of All* shows that coloring is really a mathematical rather than an artistic concept and that it has multimillion dollar industrial applications. Among other materials, this section presents a problem that has been studied for over 100 years. Some versions of the problem are easy to solve, whereas others could only be solved with the advent of computers. The basic problem is "How many colors do you need?" Students answer this question through a range of activities. There is a relatively basic activity called *The Young Map Colorer* that is an introduction to the mathematical perspective of coloring regions or countries on a map. The problem is to try to use as few colors as possible. There are on-line stories that bring the problem to life. Students can progress through this simple exercise to proof of the four-color theorem. *Untangling the Mystery of Knots* has students make and verify observations about knots to show how the study is of interest to theoretical physicists and molecular biologists. *Algorithms and Ice Cream for All* poses the problem of where to put an ice cream stand in a town so that no one person has to go too far for a treat. *Machines That Eat Your Words* deals with a finite-state machine—an imaginary machine used to design and study systems that recognize and identify patterns. *Welcome to Hotel Infinity* uses stories and concepts and allows students to illustrate an ongoing interactive story. *Games on Graphs* explores graph theory and shows how graphs are used in computer network design, urban planning, molecular biology, finding the best way to route and schedule airplanes, and even in inventing a secret code. Stories provide scenarios for games students can play on graphs. There is even an unsolved problem—if one of your students is able to solve it, they can receive a cash prize from the Hungarian mathematician, Paul Erdos. *Just a Usual Day at Unusual School* has students perform various plays that present mathematical problems and concepts. For example, in Unusual School some students always lie while the rest always tell the truth. Find out who is and is not telling the truth.

MATH WITH PHOTOGRAPHS

http://acorn.educ.nottingham.ac.uk/Maths/photomath

Take your students to the University of Nottingham for an unusual math lesson. Students may choose any of the on-site photographs to obtain a related practical math problem. For example, choosing the picture of the cactus brings the question: "The person standing next to this cactus is 160 cm. tall. How tall is the cactus?" Or, by clicking on a photograph of a honeycomb, students are asked to arrange coins in the same cell patterns.

MATHEMATICAL ANIMATION GALLERY

http://mathserv.math.sfu.ca/Animations/animations.html

Students and faculty at Simon Fraser University in Canada have used mathematical formulas to create an exhibit of animated pictures. View the formulas and pictures of such items as two linked doughnuts with one revolving around the other, a bicycle on a Sunday afternoon ride, or a rotating windmill.

PAVILION OF POLYHEDREALITY

http://www.li.net/~george/pavilion.html

This site is devoted to "practical polyhedra." Students can view real-world examples of this geometric shape while listening to "choreographed" music. Exhibits include *Nailbangers Nightmare* (a simple project for weekend carpenters), and various polyhedra constructed of paper, paper clips, and even apples and oranges. Students will be interested in the 60 forks arranged along the edges of a rhombic triacontahedron. After viewing the exhibits, take your students to the on-site library, where there are 850 polyhedra, explanations on varying levels of difficulty, and even some suggested projects and quizzes.

CHAPTER 8

History and Natural History

If you want the best information available, go right to the source. For dinosaurs and archaeological discoveries, go to the actual excavation digs. To find out about the history of modern childhood, go to England, where our modern conceptions of childhood actually began. From the Fire Fighters' Museum to the time of pillars of fire—the Dead Sea Scrolls—take your students to see original fossils, documents, and equipment. Remember that museums and galleries often change exhibits, so if you don't find exactly what you're looking for in our descriptions, you may still wish to check these sites for possibilities.

A-BOMB MUSEUM

http://www.csi.ad.jp/ABOMB/index.html

The purpose of this joint Japanese and American project, hosted in Japan, is to "provide accurate information about the impact of the . . . atomic bomb on Hiroshima" and to "provide a context for constructive discussion of what the world can learn" to ensure that such weapons of destruction are never used again. This is a powerful exhibit that includes eyewitness accounts from children, exhibits from the Peace Memorial Museum, voices of survivors, interviews, pictures of Peace Park, and movies of the Japanese Peace Memorial. There are letters from the mayor of Hiroshima and other Japanese who insist that they have a responsibility not merely to offer themselves as victims, but also to air their own atrocities. The letters from Americans span the range from apologetic to insisting that if Japan had developed the atomic bomb first, *they* would surely have used it. Although the bias of the site administrators is clearly stated, they have conscientiously presented all sides of the argument for and against the use of the atomic bomb.

AMERICAN MUSEUM OF NATURAL HISTORY

http://www.hcc.hawaii.edu/dinos/dinos.1

Honolulu Community College has an on-line exhibit of dinosaur fossils that are replicas of those at the American Museum of Natural History in New York City. With the proper computer hardware, your students can hear the narrative tour of the museum. If not, on-site written material is available along with such images as a triceratops skull, a t-rex, and a stegosaurus skeleton.

BRITISH ART AND THE ORIGINS OF MODERN CHILDHOOD

http://www.uampfa.berkeley.edu/exhibits/newchild

This site is ideal for those students who complain about having to walk to school and owning only one Nintendo machine. Through the art of Georgian England, the site traces the history of modern childhood from 1730-1830. Narratives describe the social context of the artwork in nine sections: "The Age of Innocence"; "The Georgian Family and the Parental Role"; "Childbirth and Nursery"; "Child's Play Toys and Recreation"; "The Child Learns"; "Children and Charity"; "Children, Class and Countryside"; "The Family and Sentiment"; and "When Children Aren't Children." The self-guided tour for "Young People and Their Families" asks questions that will spur some interesting classroom discussions. For example, children view a painting of wealthy children holding tools and are asked whether they think these children ever used the tools. There is also a timeline of eighteenth-century events and an interview with the exhibit's curator.

CAMBRIAN EXPLOSION

http://members.aol.com/kbclark/cambrian/index.html

This site uses 3-D computer graphics to reconstruct and show extinct life-forms through fossil extrapolation. The exhibit begins with pre-Cambrian habitats and organisms, continues through the Paleozoic seas, and concludes with modern animal forms. There is also an explanation of how the 3-D images were developed.

CHICAGO HISTORICAL SOCIETY

http://www.chicagohs.org

It isn't just about Chicago! The Chicago Historical Society is always full of surprises, which change regularly. In the fall, the featured exhibits were about Abraham Lincoln, political conventions in Chicago dating back to the 1800s, and the Great Chicago Fire. The tour makes use of the Internet in creative ways. For example, the Chicago Fire exhibit not only had photographs, texts, and reminiscences, but even a stereographic 3-D image of Chicago in ashes. The political conventions exhibition had a collection of political cartoons, photographs, and texts as well as memories of both famous and ordinary citizens. Hearing from a woman who was a teenager in 1932 when FDR was nominated and who was actually invited to sit in the Roosevelt family's private box brings history alive.

COLLEGE OF EASTERN UTAH PREHISTORIC MUSEUM

http://www.ceu.edu/museum/index.htm

Price, Utah, located 119 miles from Salt Lake City, was a playground for various dinosaurs and the Fremont people—hunter/cultivators who lived from A.D. 400 to A.D. 1300. Students can view one of the largest raptor skeletons in the world and learn about eight different dinosaurs, a mammoth, and the Fremont people.

DEAD SEA SCROLLS—LIBRARY OF CONGRESS

http://sunsite.unc.edu/expo/deadsea.scrolls.exhibit/intro.html

This site contains materials from the Library of Congress exhibition, "Scrolls from the Dead Sea: The Ancient Library of Qumran and Modern Scholarship." The exhibition describes the historical context of the scrolls and the Qumran community and relates the story of the discovery of the scrolls 2,000 years later. There are images of scroll fragments and other objects on loan from the Israel Antiquities Authority, accompanied by narratives.

DUKE PAPYRUS ARCHIVE

http://odyssey.lib.duke.edu/papyrus

The *Duke Papyrus Archive* contains texts and images of 1,373 papyri from ancient Egypt. Browse by subject or search by keyword to see the images of each papyrus, available in various magnifications. There is also extensive background material on papyri and papyrology.

For other material available in this site, see Chapter 1—African American History—Duke University Special Collections Library.

EGYPTOLOGY

http://www.sptimes.com/egypt

This site, hosted by the *St. Petersburg Times*, contains portions of an Egyptology exhibit from the International Museum in Florida. Follow the paths of kings and queens of ancient Egypt in this on-line tour. You can see photographs, take a test, and download a study guide on the lives, times, and lands of the ancients.

ELLIS ISLAND—A VIRTUAL HERITAGE MUSEUM

See Chapter 11—Schools—United States—Washington—Alderwood Elementary School—Bellingham.

EMORY UNIVERSITY MUSEUM'S ANCIENT EGYPT GALLERY

http://www.cc.emory.edu/CARLOS/egypt.gal.html

One of the surest ways of stimulating student interest in Egyptian culture is through mummies. Emory University has compiled this extensive collection of artifacts, primarily concerned with the Egyptian concept of death.

FIELD MUSEUM OF NATURAL HISTORY

http://www.fmnh.org/exhibits/Exhibits.htm

Take your students to Chicago's Field Museum, where there is an extensive exhibit on *Life over Time*. The exhibit, which consists primarily of paintings and vivid texts, is interspersed with various activities and games and even includes an animated movie about dinosaurs. Students are able to examine life from the beginning of time through the dinosaur period and into the Neanderthal and Piltdown eras. Excerpts from the teacher's guide to the exhibit are included with pre- and post-tour activities, games, and projects, such as a dinosaur flip book.

FIRE FIGHTING, HISTORY OF

http://www.globalinfo.com/noncomm/firehouse/Firehouse.HTML

The Firehouse Museum of San Diego tells the story of fire fighting through a display of equipment and memorabilia from around the world. A photographic exhibit contains images of and descriptive texts about fire-fighting equipment and paraphernalia, including uniforms, badges, patches, and helmets.

GALLERY OF THE OPEN FRONTIER AND AMERICAN HISTORY

http://www.unl.edu/UP/gof/home.htm

Take your students on a trip to the American West courtesy of the University of Nebraska. The university has compiled digital images of photographs, paintings, and drawings from materials obtained from the United States National Archives. Images include the name of the artist, the date of creation, the subject, the locale, and other information. Show your students the San Francisco Earthquake of 1905, children on the frontier, dams and canals, trains and railroads, sod houses and other homesteads, Native Americans, schools, farming, and construction projects. The project is ongoing and new topics are constantly being added.

GLENBOW

http://www.glenbow.org

Visit Glenbow, Canada's foremost center of history and art, to view historical objects and learn about the people and events that have shaped western Canada. Among several other exhibits, there is an extensive collection in the *Military History Gallery,* which focuses on European, Asian, and North American firearms and edged weapons, Japanese arms and armor, and medals, orders, and decorative associations within Canada.

HELLENIC CIVILIZATION

http://www.greekcivil.ariadne-t.gr/default.html

This site provides access to most museums located in Greece. Included in the section entitled "Historical Museums" are a variety of institutions that contain on-line exhibits of Greek statesmen, folk art, and ethnology. Additional institutions are accessible via the category "Museums of Natural History," including the Cureu Museum of Shells; the Mineralogical Museums of Kamariza and Larion; the Museum of Shells of the Greek Seas, the Nature Study and Folk Art Museum of Loutra Almopias, and the Goulandris Museum of Natural History.

For other information contained in this site, see Chapter 2—Greece.

HOLOCAUST CYBRARY

See Chapter 1—Holocaust.

ILLINOIS STATE MUSEUM

http://www.museum.state.il.us/exhibits/index.html

The Illinois State Museum in Springfield uses the Internet in novel ways to make history come alive. You can spend all day here and still not see everything. The exhibit *At Home in Springfield* covers family life in Illinois from 1700 to the present. Students choose answers that determine how a particular story unfolds, and along the way they learn much more than mere facts about the time and place they're studying. They actually become a part of the story and begin to pay attention to details of place, custom, and decor. For example, as Nicholas Chassin, a royal storekeeper, they must decide how to finish completing their home by procuring a certain "article of furniture"—an interesting classroom discussion is certain to result when they find that Nicholas is actually talking about a wife. The museum also has teacher resources for grades 3-5, 6-9, and 10-12 that cover language arts, art and geography, and social studies, as well as games and puzzles. Natural history materials include *Mazon Creek Fossils,* which shows fossils recovered from the Francis Creek Shale, and an extensive exhibit covering *The Midwestern United States 16,000 Years Ago*.

INDIANS OF THE AMERICAS

http://lark.acs.csulb.edu/gc/libarts/am-indian/index.html

This far-ranging site from California State University in Long Beach attempts to capture the entire history of Native Americans, from the Siberian exodus in the 1600s through 1990, using photographs, recordings, paintings, and texts. Included are materials on the occupation of Alcatraz Island from 1969 to 1971. *Native American Experience* is a collection of historical photographs and information arranged chronologically from the prehistoric and Paleo-Indian to 1990. The exhibit includes information and images that provide historical and cultural backgrounds of the event, person, or subject presented. *Theodore De Bry Copper Plate Engravings* is a collection of images and descriptions depicting early Native American life in the United States. *The Sound Project of Oklahoma Indians* presents the words of several tribes speaking in their native languages. There is also an *Aboriginal Art Gallery*, presenting the paintings of two Canadian Indians, and numerous links to other exhibits.

INSTITUTE OF EGYPTIAN ART AND ARCHAEOLOGY

http://www.memst.edu/egypt/main.html

The Institute of Egyptian Art and Archaeology at the University of Memphis pays homage to its ancient namesake with this exhibit of ancient Egyptian artifacts. Students can examine statues, masks, cartouches, and sarcophagi and will be especially interested in the description of how a CAT-scan of the inside of a mummy's head revealed he had died of an ear infection that spread to the brain.

For other information contained in this site, see Chapter 2—Egypt.

KELSEY MUSEUM AT THE UNIVERSITY OF MICHIGAN

http://www.umich.edu/~kelseydb

This site contains a variety of on-line exhibitions, including *Portals to Eternity* (featuring the Necropolis at Terenouthis in lower Egypt), *Wondrous Glass* (reflections on the world of Rome from 50 B.C. to A.D. 650, Roman glass making, special uses for glass, and so on), *Preserving*

Eternity (modern goals, Egyptian funerary artifacts, etc.), and exhibitions that cover Ancient Nubia, Byzantium, archaeology, ancient Greek and Roman art and artifacts, and maps of the ancient world.

LEONARDO DA VINCI MUSEUM

See Chapter 12—da Vinci, Leonardo.

LIBRARY OF CONGRESS

http://lcweb.loc.gov/homepage/lchp.html

Think of having the Library of Congress across the street from your school, with all its primary source documents, sound recordings, and videotapes. You would probably check there monthly for materials. Exhibits at the on-line Library of Congress frequently change, and even permanent on-line exhibits are always adding material, so we suggest that any time you need material pertaining to American history, literature, science, or social studies, you check here. At the front door to the LOC is "The Learning Page," which gives you information on lesson plans, an overview of the LOC, and ideas on how best to use it, and then takes you on a tutorial called "Becoming a History Detective." To give you an idea of the breadth of materials available at this site, consider the huge "American Memory" permanent exhibit. It has, among hundreds of items, original documents from the Continental Congress, manuscripts and photographs from folklore interviews and from the WPA Writers' Project, and Walt Whitman's actual notebooks and samples from his cardboard butterfly collection. Students can read or hear voices ranging from a mill worker in North Carolina to great writers.

For other information contained in this site, see Chapter 2—United States—Washington, D.C.—Library of Congress.

THE LINCOLN MUSEUM

http://www.thelincolnmuseum.org/museum_index.html

The Lincoln Museum offers a comprehensive view of the life and legacy of Abraham Lincoln and the United States during his lifetime. Various on-line galleries include *Lincoln's America*, *Prairie Politician to President*, *Civil War*, *Ford Theater*, and *Family Album*. Each of these galleries is packed with images and information. For example, *Lincoln's America* is divided into various regions of the United States. Clicking on the southern portion of the interactive U.S. map brings up not only texts but also graphics of such items as bills of sale for slaves. There is also an interactive Lincoln Quiz that can be taken on a beginner or timed advanced level.

MUSEUM OF ANTIQUITIES

http://www.ncl.ac.uk/~nantiq

Take your students to the largest museum of archaeology in northeast England, located by the University of Newcastle upon Tyne, near Hadrian's Wall. The virtual gallery of this British exhibition, *Flints and Stones: Real Life in Prehistory*, features a new object each month, with past months' objects archived on site. The presentation includes separate texts for adults and students. The exhibit examines the world of the late Stone Age hunters and gatherers of Britain and northwest Europe. Sections include *Meet the Shaman* (the leader of the Stone Age people takes you into his living world), *Meet the Archaeologist* and *Find Your Way in Time*. After taking the tour, there is a food quiz that is designed to "see if you could survive as a hunter and gatherer today by picking the right foods." There are also teachers' activities that, although tied to England's national curriculum guidelines, are readily adaptable to classes in any country. For example, using cardboard tubes and marbles, students construct their own water system, modeled after the Roman system.

MUSEUM OF CIVILIZATION

http://www.cmcc.muse.digital.ca/cmc/cmceng/welcmeng.html

The Museum of Civilization in Quebec includes on-line exhibits on bone snow knives and tin oil lamps, Christmas traditions in France and Canada, traditions among Canada's First People, the oldest longboat on the North American continent (250 years), a Chinese collection of jade, ivory, and bronze and a magnificent imperial bed, and a detailed and moving history of Quebec. Temporary exhibits have included such topics as objects and traditions of Amazonia. A new exhibit is featured each month. These will include such topics as kimonos, immigrants, soaps, and miniatures.

MUSEUM OF SINGAPORE ART AND HISTORY

http://www.museum.org.sgnas/nas.html

This on-line museum, hosted by the government of Singapore, includes exhibits from the National Archives of Singapore, the Asian Civilizations Museum, the Singapore History Museum, and the Singapore Art Museum. The National Archive holdings include public records, building plans of offices, stores, theaters, and mosques; oral history recordings, and photographs. The Asian Civilizations Museum focuses on the ancestral cultures of Singaporians and as such contains textiles, garments, and art and artifacts from southeast Asia, China, India, and the Islamic world. The history museum traces historical trends and developments that have shaped the life and history of the country through demographics, social identification, festivals, trade, and commerce.

NATIONAL ARCHIVES AND RECORDS ADMINISTRATION

http://clio.nara.gov/exhall/exhibits.html

The National Archives and Records Administration (NARA) in Washington, D.C., maintains a number of exhibits relating to American history. *Tokens and Treasures* is an exhibit of gifts given to 12 U.S. presidents by ordinary citizens and various heads of state. The *American Originals* exhibit contains some of NARA's most interesting and famous documents, including the Louisiana Purchase, a police report on the Lincoln assassination, Nixon's letter of resignation, FDR's declaration of war, and the verdict against Al Capone. Other exhibits include original copies of the Declaration of Independence and Constitution (including the rarely seen second page) and poster art from World War II. There is also a recording of the song *Any Bonds Today?* and sample articles from NARA's monthly magazine, *Prologue* (such as "Women Soldiers of the Civil War" and "The Surprising George Washington," a look at the man behind the myth).

See also Chapter 1—World War II.

NATIONAL CIVIL RIGHTS MUSEUM

http://www.mecca.org/~crights/ncrm.html

Take your students to Memphis's Civil Rights Museum, where they can learn about the long and continuing struggle for civil rights. Exhibits are arranged in chronological order from the Brown v. Board of Education of Topeka case through Martin Luther King, Jr.

See also Chapter 1—African American History.

NATIONAL MUSEUM OF JAPANESE HISTORY

See Chapter 2—Japan.

NATIONAL PARK SERVICE

http://www.cr.nps.gov/csp/treasures.html

Since its creation in 1916, the United States National Park Service has managed an extensive museum collection. There are over 28 million objects that fall under the service's purvey, as well as 14,000 linear feet of archives. This site profiles the collection and shows samples that rotate on a regular basis. View such items as historical furnishings of presidents' homes, flags that flew over Fort Sumter, Thomas Edison's notes on inventions, tools and furnishings of a working ranch in Montana, and botanical specimens from Yosemite.

ORIENTAL INSTITUTE—UNIVERSITY OF CHICAGO

http://www_oi.uchicago.edu/OI/MUS/OI-Museum.html

In the 1930s, the heyday of archaeological expeditions to the Middle East, the University of Chicago's Oriental Institute was among the leading institutions. This site contains a sample of images from the institute's photographic archives showing now-vanished temples and tombs, famed archaeologists standing by their greatest finds, and digs and artifacts. Click on the map to visit exhibitions on Egypt, Iran, Iraq, and the Sudan, or visit the site on Persepolis and ancient Iran. Your students will enjoy reading the *Mummy's Memo*, in which the mummy complains to the staff of the Oriental Institute about how current climatic conditions in the Midwest are hastening his deterioration. Students can then explore further to learn what efforts are being made to keep the mummy preserved.

PALEONTOLOGY

http://www.levins.com/hadrosaurus.html

The first dinosaur skeleton discovery, believe it or not, occurred in Haddonfield, New Jersey, in 1858 when a vacationing English fossil hobbyist overheard excavation workers talking about some giant bones they had found. The story of the Haddonfield discovery, complete with photographs and kid-friendly text, is presented by Hoag Levins, a journalist and photographer who writes a syndicated column on the Internet.

PALEONTOLOGY WITHOUT WALLS

http://www.ucmp.berkeley.edu/exhibit/exhibits.html

This University of California at Berkeley site is divided into sections on systematics, taxonomy, dinosaur discoveries, and vertebrae flights. An easy-to-use search function enables you to bypass the divisions and go directly to a more specific topic. The site includes biographies of over a dozen scientists from Aristotle and da Vinci to Paley and Wegener, many of their works, and a glossary.

ROYAL BRITISH COLUMBIA MUSEUM

http://rbcm1.rbcm.gov.bc.ca/index_rc.html

The Royal British Columbia Museum in Victoria is devoted to the natural and human history of the region. Students studying totem poles will be interested in its extensive on-line collection that, although in black and white, is presented in great detail and with clear explanations. The more extensive section of this site deals with natural history, covering current, endangered, and extinct species as well as ecology. Although geared to the British Columbia curriculum, there are many lesson plans that can be adapted to any class dealing with ecology or the natural world.

CHAPTER 9

Science and Industry

The world's most prestigious scientific laboratories and international industries have opened their virtual doors for your students. From Renaissance science to nuclear physics, from paper airplanes to space shuttles—interactive opportunities in this chapter will let students tend a garden on the other side of the world with a robotic arm, travel through the human body, ask questions of scientists around the world, and pay a visit to Hershey Foods.

See also Chapters 3 *and* 8.

INDUSTRY

Crayola Factory

http://www.crayola.com/crayola/home.html

Your students can take a tour of the Crayola factory, where they can learn how crayons and markers are manufactured, learn the history of Crayola, and take a Crayola quiz. They can learn the major ingredients of a crayon, how many it would take to reach the moon, and where the word originated.

Hershey Foods

http://www.hersheys.com/~hershey

It's safer than Willie Wonka's. The folks from Hershey will take you on a "chocolate" tour where you will learn how candy bars are made—from the gathering of cacao beans to the final molding process. You can also learn about the history of chocolate, from 200 B.C. through Milton Hershey and Hershey Foods.

SCIENCE—GENERAL

Beakman's Place

http://pomo.nbn.com/youcan

The popular television science show, *Beakman's Place*, has an online site with a variety of facts and activities. Such questions as why your feet smell and why your stomach doesn't disintegrate when it secretes hydrochloric acid are perfect for grabbing the attention of students. There are several interesting experiments with direct appeal to students. For example, *Beakman's Place* will show you how to make "mucus and boogers" with the same ingredients that your body uses—proteins and sugars. Other questions and experiments include what happens to your lungs when you smoke and why the moon seems larger when it's closer to the horizon.

Mad Scientist Network

http://medinfo.wustl.edu/~ysp/MSN

Did you ever wonder how many calories can be burned up by the brain, how quicksand actually works, or why your grandfather eventually stops growing? Wonder no more. A group of graduate and medical students at Washington University in St. Louis has established the *Mad Scientist Network*, a "cranial collective" of over 200 scientists from around the world in over 23 fields of science who will answer any question. Simply post your question, and one of the scientists will respond. Questions and answers are archived topically on site—etiquette dictates that you first read the archives to make sure your question has not already been answered. The archives are also searchable by grade level, so that third graders, for example, are able to see what other third graders around the world have been wondering about.

Mercury Project

http://www.usc.edu/dept/raiders

Perhaps your class would like to explore and help take care of a garden—along with other people from around the world. An actual garden has been set up in Austria, tended by a robotic arm that visitors are able to control from their own computers. Although it is possible to visit this site as either a guest on a guided tour or as a member (free of charge), only members can actually control the robotic arm. This is the second such project set up by the University of Southern California's Los Angeles laboratory. The first, which combined robotics and archaeology in an interactive installation, was the first system that allowed World Wide Web users to remotely view and alter the real world via tele-robotics. Users excavated artifacts buried in a soil-filled terrarium in USC's laboratory. People from around the world were able to work collectively to identify an unnamed ancient text in the terrarium by describing their findings and hypotheses in an ongoing operator's log. Your students can read the archives of this former project as well as tend the current garden. New projects are periodically added, so even if gardening isn't your passion (or in your curriculum), you may wish to check this site to see what the newest project is.

The Why Files

http://whyfiles.news.wisc.edu

The Why Files, a project of the National Institute for Science Education, allows electronic exploration of the science behind the news. New features are added twice a month, and files are maintained from prior features. The site explores the science of daily life, from outer space to cellular biology to the statistics of political polling. Issues addressed in the past include the relationship between eyesight and diet, spinal cord injuries, life on Mars, and nicotine addiction.

SCIENCE—THE HUMAN BODY

The Brain

http://weber.u.washington.edu/~chudler/neurok.html

Take your students on a tour of the human brain and spinal cord hosted by Professor Eric Chudler, a research assistant professor in the Department of Anesthesiology at the University of Washington in Seattle. Chudler has included a long list of activities and games to help students learn about their senses, perceptions, and neurophysiology. He will even take your students on an Internet neuroscience treasure hunt. In addition to the activities, Chudler provides a standard bibliography as well as links to on-line articles and books pertaining to the brain and spinal cord.

Cells Alive

http://www.cellsalive.com

See what happens on a cellular level when you visit this site. With photographs, movies, and animations, a variety of phenomena are explored, from the battle waged between bacteria and white and red blood cells around a splinter, to how HIV infiltrates the cells.

The Muscular System

http://www.danke.com/Orthodoc

The Muscle Page for Kids, sponsored by a legitimate massage clinic, has illustrations and information about how every major muscle and group of muscles work. There are posture tests and hints for developing and maintaining better posture and muscle tone.

The Respiratory System

http://galen.med.Virginia.EDU/~smb4v/tutorials/asthma/asthma1.html

Asthma is increasing so rapidly among our children that one New York doctor has called the situation an epidemic. Children with asthma, as well as their parents and classmates, will want to take a virtual trip to the Children's Medical Center at the University of Virginia, where they can learn all about asthma and the respiratory system through easy-to-understand texts, pictures, movies, and sounds. By clicking on pictures of kids with asthma, students can hear what they feel like when they have an attack, watch a movie showing what normal breathing looks like, and hear normal and abnormal breathing through a stethoscope. There is also a detailed section on the types of treatment available.

SCIENCE—MATERIALS SCIENCE

Microworld

http://www.lbl.gov/MicroWorlds

This interactive tour of the Lawrence Berkeley National Laboratory's Advanced Light Source is geared towards high school students. Students can learn about materials science through the latest research. They will be able to find out what the Advanced Light Source is and how this machine works, what polymers are and why they are useful, how infinitesimal quantities of trace elements can change a material, how scientists make machines that can fit through the eye of a needle, and how materials science helps in understanding environmental problems. Problem are posed with clues that encourage students to take facts and speculate further. For example, the section on selenium poses the question of how wetlands may have become contaminated with selenium and how they can be cleaned up. In Clue #1, students are told about selenium's properties and asked what uses they can think of for selenium. Subsequent clues guide them along the problem and solution trail.

SCIENCE—MUSEUMS—AVIATION AND AEROSPACE

See also Science—General, *above, and various entries in* Chapter 4.

Calgary Aerospace Museum

http://www.lexicom.ab.ca/~aerospace/aerospace.html

The Calgary Aerospace Museum has dozens of photographs of military planes from World War I to the present, as well as civilian planes, helicopters, and airplane engines. There is also information about the history of the aerospace industry and world events.

Canadian Warplane Heritage Museum

http://www.warplane.com/hub.html

This exhibit covers Canada's aviation history and includes a display of aircraft from World War II to the jet age. There are over 25 vintage Warbirds, including all of Canada's Victoria Cross Memorial aircraft.

International Women's Air and Space Museum

http://www.infinet.com/~iwasm

The International Women's Air and Space Museum in Centerville, Ohio, pays tribute to female pilots and astronauts who have made history. Through photographs and biographies, your students can learn about such women as Madame Blanchard, Napoleon's Chief Air Minister of Ballooning; Brave Bessie Coleman, the world's first female African American pilot; the World War II Women's Air Force Service Pilots Unit; women who have broken the sound barrier; and American and Russian astronauts.

National Air and Space Museum, Smithsonian Institution

http://www.nasm.si.edu

What better way to tour the Smithsonian's National Air and Space Museum than without crowds? Just enter the virtual museum, look at the floor plan, and click on the gallery you choose to visit. See the controversial Enola Gay exhibit, exhibits on World War I and II, the Apollo exhibit, and *Beyond the Limits*, an exhibit explaining and showing the role of digital computers in flight. There are also special on-line exhibits, such as *How Things Fly*, which includes dozens of simple experiments you can use in your classroom. The experiments illustrate the different qualities of air and their role in flight and propulsion.

For other information contained in this site, see Chapter 4—National Air and Space Museum, Smithsonian Institution.

San Diego Aerospace Museum

http://www.AerospaceMuseum.org

Take your students on an illustrated tour of the history of aviation, from da Vinci's sketches through space travel. Students will be able to meet the engineers, pilots, and industrialists instrumental in aerospace history. There is also a section that shows the process of airplane restoration.

United States Air Force Museum

http://www.wpafb.af.mil/museum

Take your students to Wright-Patterson Air Force Base in Ohio for a tour of the history of Air Force aviation. Personnel will provide you with English-, Spanish-, German-, or French-speaking tour guides. The *Virtual Tours Gallery* includes pictures of the Huffman Prairie Flying Field (where the Wright Brothers developed their skills), Century Series Fighters, World War II USAAF and foreign aircraft, the presidential aircraft collection, and the Lockheed Advanced Development Department (watch your students to make sure they don't take pictures of anything highly sensitive). The *Discovery Hangar*, designed for students in grades 3 to 12, explains the four principles of flight and how a jet engine works. The museum's organization and terminology can be a bit confusing. For example, the *History Gallery* is divided into eras of flight and although there is interesting information on such celebrities as Clark Gable, Jimmy Stewart, Joe Louis, and Ronald Reagan, it's difficult to find if you don't know when they served in the military.

Virtual Museum of the Invention of the Airplane

http://hawaii.cogsci.uiuc.edu/invent/air_main.shtml

Take your students back to the early, innocent days of the invention of flight via this extensive collection of photographs, articles, and movies. Be sure to visit the *Digital Library*, a collection of flight-related articles from the time of da Vinci to 1909. The articles, searchable by date, author, or title, include copies of the *Aeronautical Manual* from as far back as 1895. Stop by the *Gallery of Inventors* and meet dozens of people instrumental in aviation. Your students are certain to enjoy the movies, which include several early films of the Wright Brothers' airplanes and other pioneering flying machines. The airplane database is one of the most extensive we've found.

SCIENCE—MUSEUMS—GENERAL

Australian National Science and Technology Museum

http://sunsite.anu.edu.au/Questacon

The Australians have established this interesting interactive science museum especially for children. Be sure to visit *Kidspace,* which has interactive activities involving dinosaurs, including an illustrated story about a dinosaur that walks into a modern city—students are asked to finish the story. Be sure not to miss the *Hands On Zone,* which has several experiments. Your students will enjoy *A Stirring Sight*, *Up and Up and Away with Bottles*, and *Musical Coathangars*.

Boston Museum of Science

http://www.mos.org

Choose the path *Museum Exhibits/Online Exhibits* for a variety of exhibits. As we went to press, there were three major exhibits. *Big Dig* takes you on an archaeological and historical tour of Boston's Spectacle Island. Through brief on-line movies, photographs, and text, students learn about artifacts that have been uncovered and how they are used to piece together history. The *Theater of Electricity* teaches students about static and current electricity through text, dramatic movies, and photographs of the world's largest insulated De Graf generator. *Dance of Chance*, a collaboration between the Center for Polymer Studies and Boston University Museum of Science, uses enlarged microscopic photographs to show students how random patterns in nature result in patterns of beauty.

Buffalo Museum of Science

http://drew.buffalo.k12.ny.us/drew/ImageMap/Museum/Tour/MuseumTour.html

Take a tour of the Buffalo Museum of Science with students from the Dr. Charles R. Drew Science Magnet School in Buffalo, New York. The students will lead you through the Hall of Vertebrae, the Hall of Space, and other areas of the museum.

Franklin Institute Science Museum

http://sln.fi.edu

The Franklin Institute Science Museum will be of interest to middle, intermediate, and high school students. There are several extensive online exhibits, including *The Heart: An Online Exploration*, *Ben Franklin: Glimpses of the Man*, and *An Inquirer's Guide to the Universe*. Past exhibitions have covered the Olympics, "Your Summer Vacation on Mars," nature hikes, and science fairs. The museum's public library is also worth a visit to have students view science news, activities, and resources. The local expert is available 24 hours a day to answer e-mail questions.

Invention Dimension

http://web.mit.edu/invent

Invention Dimension is hosted by the Massachusetts Institute of Technology. Each month, a different American inventor is highlighted. Information includes a biographical sketch covering the inventor's accomplishments and the inventions impacts on society. There is an extensive archive covering a wide historical range, from Ben Franklin to Steve Jobs and Steve Wozniak of Apple Computer.

Nanoworld

http://www.uq.oz.au/nanoworld/nanohome.html

The Centre for Microscopes and Microanalysis at the University of Queensland will take you on a tour of the microscopic world. The center is dedicated to the understanding of the structure and composition of all atomic, molecular, cellular, and macromolecular scales. Students will be able to see the world from a different perspective as they see and learn about blood cells, bone marrow, and other material structures. The magnified mosquito is on par with any of the horror movies today's children seem to love so much—only it is far more informative and educational. The *Virtual Electronic Microscope* is an interactive on-site tool through which students can view the Queensland fruit fly and other exhibits. There is an extensive section on how microscopes are used in the manufacture of circuits.

Nikola Tesla Exhibit

See Chapter 12—Tesla, Nikola.

Ontario Science Centre

http://www.osc.on.ca

The Ontario Science Centre features several interactive exhibits. Students can use the center's "computer crayons" to see how paint and crayons work by taking colors away from white paper. They can also learn about the art of camouflage, feel the confusion of the "Stroop Effect," and even experience "The Marvelous Exploding Zit."

Optical Illusions

http://www.illusionworks.com

Can we really be certain of what we are seeing? Can perception differ from reality? Visit the *Optical Illusion Collection* and find out the answers to these questions while viewing pictographic and three-dimensional distortions, stereograph illusions, and color contrast effects.

http://www.grand-illusions.com

Visit this site and see optical illusions, scientific toys, visual effects, and even a little magic. Discover some of the secrets of the magic mirror, learn about and see optical illusions, including the moon—one of the most famous illusions. Stated simply, the full moon, when just above the horizon, appears much larger than when it is directly overhead. This site shows this phenomenon and discusses the problems it presents for photographers. Meet a "Professor of Illusion"—Richard Gregory, emeritus professor of neuropsychology at the University of Bristol, who presents *An Introduction to Seeing*. You might also want to see *Tim's Wonderful Toys*. Tim Rowett collects extraordinary toys and novelties, gadgets and inventions, and optical and topological devices. In fact, he's got all 7,000 of his toys in 95 suitcases, some of which he will share with you. You'll be interested in the Chinese Singing Bowl, Dual Art wooden sculptures, and his magic Mickey. Tim will not only show you his toys, but also explain how and why they work. This site usually includes an interesting feature article, such as *The Strange Story of Napoleon's Wallpaper*.

Perpetual Motion Page

http://manor.york.ac.uk/htdocs/perpetual/perpetual.html

Richard G. Clegg, of York in the United Kingdom, invites you to view his collection of perpetual motion machines, including the underwater swimming donut. Each machine comes with a diagram and an explanation of how it works. There is also an explanation of how each machine does not work—because, as everyone knows, there is no such thing as perpetual motion.

San Francisco Exploratorium

http://www.exploratorium.edu

The San Francisco Exploratorium is one of the oldest Internet hands-on museums and a perennial favorite of teachers. Although teachers are used to thinking of the Exploratorium in terms of science, changing exhibitions may include such events as *Remembering Nagasaki* and an interview with Robert McKimmie of the California Historical Society. The topics of on-line exhibits may range from vocal cords (what happens when you give someone "the raspberries") to the Hubble telescope, and from mutant fruit flies to optical illusions—images that seem to fade, shimmer, or change colors the longer you stare at them. This is an extensive site, with an organization that often seems serendipitous, so leave yourself time to explore. Some of the projects, such as Project Link, a real-time on-line video conference with scientists on board a plane, require considerable advance planning. The Exploratorium also presents projects and experiments that have been developed by teachers, such as building a fog chamber and studying the Doppler effect.

Saskatchewan Science Centre

http://www.sciencecentre.saskweb.com/main/library.html

Take your students to Canada to learn and have fun at this interactive science museum. The on-line science lab has hundreds of simple classroom experiments, searchable by subject or by the name of the experiment. Your students will be intrigued by the on-line optical illusions. For example, after staring at a black dot inside of an on-screen flag they are instructed to click on the flag to make it disappear. Watch their amazement when their eyes still see the outline of the flag around the dot. Each optical illusion comes with an explanation of why the eye misperceives. Students can also view 3-D stereograms and participate in such simple science craft projects as building a balloon rocket car or making a glow-in-the-dark star chart. There is also an interactive periodic table of elements and a scientific trivia game in which students choose the level of difficulty and play for computer-simulated tokens.

Science Museum of London

http://www.nmsi.ac.uk

Collections and galleries in the Science Museum of London include a collection of objects that helped shape the modern world—from genetically engineered mice to Charles Babbage's calculating engines. Students enter the exhibit through the virtual front door and are presented with a floor plan showing the various exhibits they are able to visit. Choices include *The Science of Art and Medicine; Heat and*

Temperature; Optics; Science in the Eighteenth Century; Glimpses of Medical History; Flight; Chemistry; Nuclear Physics; Agriculture; Marine Engineering and Shipping; Telecommunications; Time Measurement; Power; Space; Land Transportation; Secret Life of the Home; Fire Fighting; Roads, Bridges and Tunnels, and so on. Although the organization of this site is somewhat confusing, there is an on-line search function that may be used to find things that aren't readily apparent. For example, we located an intriguing selection of optical illusions via the search function that we couldn't locate by wandering through the museum.

"The Yuckiest Site on the Internet"

http://www.nj.com/yucky/index.html

This site is proudly proclaimed to be "The Yuckiest Site on the Internet" because it focuses on scientific topics of gross interest, such as the inside of a cow's eye. When we last checked, the main exhibit was on cockroaches. Dr. Betty Faber, "the bug lady," uses creativity, facts, and activities to teach how cockroaches live, what their habits are, and how to get rid of them. Students can view a giant roach and then click on any body part and see how it works. They may also study a world map showing the homes of various species and read about a "Day in the Life" of a roach named Rodney. There is also a forum where students are able to swap roach tales. We suggest that you monitor this part because both the organization and content tend to get a bit out of control.

SCIENCE—MUSEUMS—HISTORY

Faces of African Americans in the Sciences

http://www.lib.lsu.edu/lib/chem/display/faces.html

Louisiana State University (LSU) invites your class to their exhibit, which profiles African American men and women who have contributed to the advancement of science and engineering. There are dozens of biographies of African American scientists, doctors, and inventors, complete with pictures and bibliographies. The materials are arranged alphabetically by last name and discipline.

History of the Microscope

http://www.utmem.edu/personal/thjones/hist/hist_mic.htm

Thomas Jones, a graduate of Duke University's School of Medicine, has put together this exhibit, which covers the history of the light microscope, from the use of a simple lens in ancient times to the first compound microscope circa 1590, to nineteenth-century instruments. There are 50 images of major types of microscopes, styles, makers, and users. This is primarily a textual site, with minimal graphics.

History of Pharmacy Museum

http://www.pharm.arizona.edu/museum/page1.html

This tour of the University of Arizona's History of Pharmacy Museum covers both pharmacology and Americana. Students will see and learn about glass globes (similar to barber poles), and how red globes warned strangers that there was an epidemic, whereas green globes meant the town was safe. (See if your students can trace the connection of the globes to modern traffic lights.) Among other exhibits are collections of jars and bottles (including a cod liver oil bottle shaped like a fish), pestles, syringes, medicine chests and cabinets, punchboards, pinball and slot machines, and a jar containing pieces of John Dillinger's chewing gum (not manufactured or endorsed by Dillinger, but rather chewed by him).

Institute and History of Science Museum of Florence, Italy

http://galileo.imss.firenze.it/index.html

This on-line museum, with materials in both English and Italian, has approximately 20 objects, including the right middle finger of Galileo. Visit the *Multimedia Catalog of Galileo's Room*, a virtual visit with descriptions of the artifacts on display, biographical materials, and detailed texts that offer a more complete understanding of the historical-scientific context of such artifacts as telescopes, compasses, and magnets. Each text is accompanied by still or animated images or filmed sequences.

Renaissance Science

http://bang.lanl.gov/video/stv/arshtml/lanlarstitle.html

Two professors at the City University of New York have put together a history of Renaissance science with an emphasis on Galileo and mathematics. Illustrations include original pages from Galileo's works. To make the subject more interesting, students are able to listen to Renaissance music while viewing the materials.

Women in Science

http://www.astr.ua.edu/4000WS

This site from the University of Alabama reminds us that although the first scientist recorded in literature was male (the architect of the pyramids), the second, 4,000 years ago, was female. Learn about her and dozens of subsequent women scientists and inventors by visiting this site. Biographies are organized both alphabetically and chronologically. There is also an interactive quiz based upon materials contained in the on-site biographical sketches. Winners receive a certificate and, if they grant permission, their names will be archived in the on-site Hall of Fame.

SCIENCE—MUSEUMS—HOLOGRAPHY

http://www.holoworld.com

Frank DeFreitas, who owns a hologram gallery in Allentown, Pennsylvania, has set up this award-winning *Internet Webseum of Holography*. DeFreitas is especially interested in working with students and teachers, and to that end, he not only has free on-line workshops, but, due to teacher requests, also holds off starting until October so that teachers have organizational time at the beginning of the school year. In addition to "attending" the workshops, you can download movies showing how lasers work and how holograms are made, see laser light shows and demonstrations of optic principles, and view laser experiments. There is also a series of holograph and laser videos, which includes a glossary, step-by-step diagrams showing how holograms are made, and an introduction to holography. Mr. DeFreitas has even included a separate section that explains holograms to younger children.

SCIENCE—PALEONTOLOGY

See Chapter 8—Paleontology *and* Paleontology Without Walls.

SCIENCE—PHYSICS

See also Science—General, *above.*

Fermilab

http://www.fnal.gov

The Fermilab in suburban Chicago is a high-energy physics laboratory and home of the Tevatron—the world's most powerful particle accelerator. Scientists from around the world use Fermilab's resources to explore fundamental particles and the forces of nature. Now your students can also visit the laboratory and learn about high-energy physics and tour the accelerators.

For other information on this site, see Chapter 3—Bird Watching—Birds of Fermilab.

FusEdWeb

http://fusedweb.pppl.gov

Your students can learn about fusion energy from the staff at the Princeton Plasma Physics Lab. The site, directed towards junior high and high school students, includes science modules for classroom use or independent study, teacher and student resource guides, and e-mail access to fusion energy experts. Students are invited to submit their own materials for review and publication. A related site for fifth graders to grad students, Internet Plasma Physics EXperience, is available at: http://ippex.pppl.gov/ippex.

CHAPTER 10

Libraries and Resource Centers

One of the Internet's greatest achievements may well be libraries where you don't have to keep your students quiet. Whether you're looking for the traditional works, reference materials, specialty works, such as reproductions of Dante and Ovid, or special collections on any particular subject, you'll want to browse this chapter.

ATLANTIC MONTHLY

See Chapter 5—Poetry Readings.

AUSTEN, JANE

http://uts.cc.utexas.edu/~churchh/janeinfo.html

In addition to compiling almost everything Austen ever wrote—from novels to poems to letters—this site includes biographical materials, scholarly articles, pictures (including the Austen family coat of arms), a map of England showing Austen landmarks, links to other Austen resources, and even a list of the top Jane Austen songs (based upon the characters in her novels).

BARTLEBY LIBRARY

http://www.columbia.edu/acis/bartleby

Columbia University's on-line library provides access to a variety of nineteenth- and twentieth-century works, filed alphabetically by author. There are a variety of fiction and nonfiction works, as well as a copy of *Bartlett's Quotations*.

BLAKE, WILLIAM

http://jefferson.village.virginia.edu/blake

This electronic archive, perhaps the most ambitious Blake project ever attempted, is sponsored by the Library of Congress in conjunction with the University of Virginia. When completed, the archive will contain original copies of every one of Blake's books—many of them never reproduced before—supplemented by paintings, drawings, and commercial illustrations. Eventually, the collection will contain approximately 3,000 images, indexed by subject, dates, and themes.

CHILDREN'S CLASSIC LITERATURE

http://www.ucalgary.ca/~dkbrown/storclas.html

This site contains a large collection of children's classic literature, including works by Louisa May Alcott, L. Frank Baum, Lewis Carroll, Charles Dickens, Sir Arthur Conan Doyle, Nathaniel Hawthorne, O. Henry, Washington Irving, Rudyard Kipling, Lucy Maud Montgomery, Robert Louis Stevenson, Booth Tarkington, Jules Verne, H. G. Wells, and Oscar Wilde. Many of the works have photographs and some have sound files. There is also a copy of *Young Visitors*, described as the world's only best-seller written by an eight year old. You can search for a book by either author or title.

CHILDREN'S STORYBOOKS ONLINE

See Chapter 13—Children's Storybooks Online.

COLORING BOOKS

See Chapter 13—Carlos' Coloring Book, Kendra's Coloring Book, *and* Pooh's Page.

DANTE

http://www.nd.edu/~italnet/Dante

Notre Dame University, in collaboration with the University of Chicago, invites your students to view selected pages from original editions of Dante's *Divine Comedy*, complete with woodcuts. These are excerpts from the *Renaissance Dante in Print* collection at the University of Notre Dame, which is considered one of the top ten Renaissance collections in North America.

DISNEY INTERACTIVE STORYBOOKS

See Chapter 13—Disney Interactive Storybooks.

DUKE UNIVERSITY SPECIAL COLLECTIONS LIBRARY

http://odyssey.lib.duke.edu

Take your students to the special collections library at Duke University, which focuses on human experience and culture through primary source materials. Much of the material is scanned rather than transcribed, so your students can see the originals exactly as they look. Exhibits change frequently so you may want to visit the library periodically. Examples of permanent (and expanding) exhibits include a collection of Greek manuscripts, writings by famous women, and documents from American slavery.

See also Chapter 1—African American History.

DWIGHT D. EISENHOWER PRESIDENTIAL LIBRARY

See Chapter 12—Eisenhower, Dwight David.

FRANKLIN DELANO ROOSEVELT LIBRARY

See Chapter 12—Roosevelt, Franklin Delano, and Eleanor Roosevelt.

GEORGE BUSH PRESIDENTIAL LIBRARY

See Chapter 12—Bush, George, and Barbara Bush.

GERALD FORD PRESIDENTIAL LIBRARY

See Chapter 12—Ford, Gerald.

GET LOST ADVENTURE MAGAZINE

http://www.itsnet.com/home/getlost/mag.html

This magazine, available only in electronic form, is dedicated to the more extreme sports, such as mountain biking, rock climbing, skiing, and snowboarding. The publishers contend that "A ship in the harbor is safe. But that's not what ships are built for." Students will be able to vicariously experience these sports through on-line stories and information.

HARRY S. TRUMAN LIBRARY

See Chapter 12—Truman, Harry S., and Bess Truman.

HERBERT HOOVER LIBRARY

See Chapter 12—Hoover, Herbert.

HOLOCAUST CYBRARY

See Chapter 1—Holocaust.

ILLUSTRATED WORKS OF OVID

http://www.uvm.edu/~hag/ovid/index.html

The University of Vermont's Rare Book Department owns an extensive collection of the illustrated works of Ovid. Included are several editions of *The Metamorphosis* with engravings by the seventeenth-century German artist Johann Wilhelm Baur, depicting 150 scenes from the work. Each engraving has a brief description in German and Latin and is accompanied by English text. Examples of the university's holdings are contained on site.

JIMMY CARTER PRESIDENTIAL LIBRARY

See Chapter 12—Carter, Jimmy, and Rosalynn Carter.

LIBRARY OF CONGRESS

http://lcweb.loc.gov/homepage/lchp.html

This is one of the most extensive sites that we have found on the Internet. Your students will be able to tour the Washington, D.C., Library of Congress and its exhibits that focus on American history. If you are looking for a specific exhibit, use the on-line search function. If not, you are sure to find something of interest by simply wandering through the facility. Most of the topics pertaining to American history are located in the path *American Memory*.

For more detailed information, see Chapter 1—African American History, World War I, *and* World War II, *and* Chapter 8—Library of Congress.

LIFE MAGAZINE

http://pathfinder.com/Life/lifehome.html

Visit *Life* magazine at the electronic newsstand. Your class will be able to find excerpts from the current issue of the magazine, search back issues, send e-mail to the editors, and read others' e-mail messages. You may want to pay a daily visit to the *Photo of the Day* and the *Today in History* exhibits. Your students will enjoy wandering through the galleries that feature *Life's* 60 classic covers and its 60 "wackiest" covers. They may also wish to visit the gallery of 1960s and 1970s photographs of the Beatles with 1990 shots of the surviving members of the band taken by Linda McCartney.

See also Photojournalism, *below, and* Chapter 6—Photography and Photojournalism.

MARTINDALE'S REFERENCE DESK

http://www-sci.lib.uci.edu/HSG/Ref.html

If your students aren't interested in the traditional reference library, perhaps they'll enjoy this extensive electronic one that includes maps, translation dictionaries, encyclopedias, scientific tables and databases, and other reference materials. The site even provides access to a multitude of on-line calculators from the simple abacus to the most sophisticated financial and mathematical tools.

NATIONAL ATLAS OF CANADA

http://www-nais.ccm.emr.ca/schoolnet

This site, available in both English and French, is the place to visit if you are looking for a Canadian map. Dozens of thematic maps are available, including topographic, demographic, historical, and even maps of air pollution and earthquakes. An interactive mapping tool enables students to construct their own maps based upon statistics and other data available on site. Students can select rivers, lakes, boundaries, and other features that allow the examination of Canadian issues, such as aging population, language, natural hazards, and wildlife. There is also an interactive Canadian geography quiz (with random questions, so that each quiz is different), a digital atlas of Canadian communities that allows students to show their perceptions of the communities in which they live, geographical facts about Canada, and teaching resources. If you don't find the information you are looking for, you can "Ask the Harkster," who is known as the master of Canadian geography. "As far as we know," says the site's administrator, "nobody has ever stumped the Harkster with any questions concerning the geography of Canada."

ONLINE LITERATURE LIBRARY

http://www.literature.org/Works

This site contains illustrated classics from such authors as Darwin, Descartes, Poe, Shelley, Stoker, Twain, Voltaire, and Wells.

ONLINE OPERA LIBRARY

http://www.nycopera.com/libmenu.html

The *OnLine Opera Library* is a great source for opera synopses, composer biographies, librettos, and images from such productions as *The Magic Flute*. To spur interest in the subject, hosts have included an online quiz. Answers can be found within the library's resources and winners are announced on site.

See also Chapter 5—Operas and Operettas.

PHOTOJOURNALISM

http://www.f8.com

This site, hosted by Focal Point, a photojournalist group, features real-time, on-line interactive photojournalism. A range of topics are covered. For example, "Saigon on Wheels" details a journey through Vietnam's motorbike culture by *National Geographic* photographer Ed Kashi, and "Russian Chronicles" follows a 5,000-mile, two-month journey across Russia by photographer Gary Matoso and writer Lisa Dicky. With a high-resolution digital camera and laptop computers, Matoso and Dicky recorded their stories and relayed them to the magazine via e-mail. The tone of many of the features will appeal to students. For example, in the feature on Cologne, Germany, photographers stop to interview teenagers.

THE POP-UP WORLD OF ANN MONTANARO

http://www.libraries.rutgers.edu/rulib/spcol/montanar/p-ex.htm

The Pop-Up World of Ann Montanaro contains a history of pop-up and movable books, as well as on-line photographs and illustrations. The exhibition was created and is maintained by Rutgers University Library.

PRESIDENTIAL LIBRARIES

See various entries in Chapter 12.

PRIMARY GRADE BOOKS

See Chapter 13 *for primary-level sites.*

SCRIPTS

http://script-o-rama.com

Are you looking for a way to enhance your students' interest in reading? The extensive collection of television and movie scripts at this site covers a variety of genres, from current popular television shows, such as *The Animaniacs* and *Caroline in the City,* to classic movies. We suggest you supervise student use of this site as unknown authors are allowed to contribute material. However, if you stay within the television and movie categories, you will avoid inappropriate material.

SMITHSONIAN PHOTOGRAPHIC LIBRARY

http://photo2.si.edu

The Smithsonian archives contain hundreds of photographs (accompanied by textual information) covering a wide variety of topics. Exhibits include a salute to the cinema, a slide show of award-winning photographs taken by Smithsonian Institution photographers, underwater photographs, and various Washington D.C. exhibits (cherry blossoms in bloom, the Washington Monument, the Vietnam Veterans Memorial, seldom seen monuments, the Million Man March, etc.). Other exhibits cover fireworks with information on the best way to photograph them, deadly Pacific sea snakes, lunar landings, the renovation of First Ladies Hall, Kayapo Indian headdresses, butterflies, the jungle canopy in Pana, dinosaurs, Chief Justice Warren Burger's funeral, green sea turtles in Costa Rica, the Clinton inaugural, what things are made of and why, and Ron Brown's funeral.

SPORTS ILLUSTRATED FOR KIDS

http:/pathfinder.com/SIFK/index.html

Archives of past stories from *Sports Illustrated for Kids* are available at this site. Stories cover a variety of topics, including interviews with professional athletes (especially teenagers), things athletes do for good luck, and tips from professionals. There are electronic polls that ask such questions as, "Is there too much stress on teenage tennis pros?" Fun features include photographs, jigsaw puzzles, opportunities for students to e-mail their questions (for example, "Why isn't women's pole vaulting an Olympic event?") , and pictures for which kids can e-mail their own captions. Be warned: Because this is essentially a commercial site, it's possible that by including the requested personal information along with the e-mail, students will end up on a mailing list. Inclusion of the information, however, is optional.

TALES OF WONDER

http://itpubs.ucdavis.edu/richard/tales

Students can read folk and fairy tales from around the world contained in this collection of stories from Russia, Siberia, Central Asia, China, Japan, the Middle East, Scandinavia, Scotland, England, Africa, India, etc.

TREASURES FROM THE SAXON STATE LIBRARY

http://lcweb.loc.gov/exhibits/dres/dresintr.html

The Saxon State Library was founded in 1556 when Prince Elector Augustus started a system to acquire books and literary works. Until 1990 the holdings in the library were behind the Iron Curtain and thus virtually inaccessible. Now your students can take a tour of the great exhibitions of engraving, incunabula, bookbinding, and design that stretch from medieval and Renaissance times through Goethe. The on-line collection includes a series of detailed texts on the history of the Saxon State Library and its various holdings, including a copy of Luther's translation of the Bible, the thirteenth-century text "Moses and the Ten Commandments," an early Latin Gospel, a Boccaccio, and many other medieval and Renaissance manuscripts. Texts are accompanied by richly detailed graphics of cover pages and other illustrations.

221 B. BAKER STREET (HOLMES' PLACE)

http://www3.nf.sympatico.ca/dave.pack/holmes.html

A dedicated Sherlock Holmes fan is compiling the complete collection of Sherlock Holmes stories, complete with illustrations and readings from such famous actors as Basil Rathbone. This is a work in progress, and currently all short stories have been completed.

CHAPTER 11

On-Line Classes and Schools

Now there's no need for inclement weather or high fees to stop anyone from learning languages, crafts, music, and dance—they're available right on the Internet. And while you're here, why not stop in classrooms around the world and see what other teachers and students are doing? Out of hundreds of school web pages, we've chosen the ones that we think offer unique information or use the Internet in the newest and most interesting ways.

ARTS AND CRAFTS CLASSES

Aunt Annie's Crafts Page

http://www.auntannie.com

Aunt Annie is waiting for your class to visit her craft shop. Each week new crafts are featured that are often tied into seasonal events. Weekly projects in October, for example, included Halloween sun catchers (or moonlight catchers) and masks. Each craft has a variety of designs to choose from, patterns, and easy-to-follow instructions. In addition to the weekly projects, there is an extensive collection at Aunt Annie's Craft Exchange, which is searchable by month, project name, or keyword. Projects are rated from easy to hard and include recipes for food, finger paints, transfer ink, modeling dough and papier-mâché, as well as instructions for pop-up greeting cards, paper-fold snowflakes, a variety of circus theme projects, geometric playthings (which teach geometry basics while creating such things as gift boxes), homemade bubbles, yard and garden ornaments, puppets, and much more.

Cartooning

http://www.worldchat.com/public/jhish/cartoon.html

Jerry Hish, a Canadian cartoonist, has created a friendly site in which he shares some of his techniques for cartoon drawing. Step-by-step illustrated instructions will take your students through drawing a cartoon lion, alligator, gorilla, and elephant. Hish provides a list of supplies and includes instructions for students to send in their works for inclusion in an on-line exhibition.

Origami

See also Chapter 2—Japan—On-line Guided Tour.

http://www.datt.co.jp/Origami

Mr. Joseph Wu tells us that the word for the art of paper folding comes from the Japanese words "oru" (to fold) and "kami" (paper). This site contains on-line galleries of origami art as well as extensive information, including a history of paper folding, how to backcoat and wet fold paper, information on washi (Japanese homemade paper), and book reviews. There are detailed instructions and diagrams for various origami figures, including seals, toads, and a jumping frog.

Pumpkin Carving

http://www.chaco.com/~glenn/jack

Students who are afraid of "sharp knives and pumpkin guts" may wish to do some on-line pumpkin carving. They can choose the features they want their pumpkin to have from an extensive menu, and the results of the carved pumpkin are then displayed on line in 3-D. Keep your students away from creator Glenn Crocker's on-site biography, which is on a separate page.

COOKING—FRENCH

See Chapter 2—France—Le Cordon Bleu Cooking School.

LANGUAGE LESSONS

Australian

See Chapter 2—Australia.

Bangla

See Chapter 2—Bangladesh.

Cree Language Lessons

http://arpp.carleton.ca/cree

Here is your chance to learn the Cree language, which is spoken in many parts of north central Alberta, Saskatchewan, and Manitoba and in northern Ontario and Quebec. On-site materials include syllabics, pronunciation, greetings and polite phrases, numbers, comments on the weather, animal words, etc. There are also on-line stories and poems.

Inuit

See Chapter 2—Canada—Leo Ussak School—Canadian Arctic.

Japanese

See Chapter 2—Japan—On-line Guided Tour.

Spanish

See Chapter 2—Spain.

MUSIC AND DANCE INSTRUCTION

Composers in Electronic Residence

http://www.edu.yorku.ca/CIERmain.html

Students interested in composing will want to spend time in cyberspace residence at Canada's York University. Students, music teachers, and composers in the United States, Canada, Japan, and Europe meet in cyberspace to share their latest compositions via sound files and to offer critiques of each other's works. The feedback is supportive and honest. You can share in this process by hearing past submissions and reading hints, comments, and critiques, and of course you're also welcome to join right in. Composers in Electronic Residence (CIER) is small, having only recently started, but it is expected to grow.

Guitar Lessons

http://www.harmony-central.com/Guitar/instruction.html

Students can learn a variety of guitar styles, theory, and techniques on line, including blues, scale harmonization and chord construction, scales, and chord development. Styles range from the relatively mundane to heavy metal, so all tastes can be accommodated.

Piano Lessons

http://www.swv.ie/tono/index.htm

Music teachers can visit the teacher's lounge while students take these beginner's piano lessons. Students can hear the notes as they play.

Pow Wow Dancing

http://www2.scsn.net/users/pgowder/dancing.htm

Learn about and see various styles of pow wow dancing. There is even a section on pow wow etiquette.

SCHOOLS—AUSTRALIA

Bushnet

http://www.bushnet.qld.edu.au/schools.htm

Several Australian schools can be accessed via this site. The schools are scattered across 6,000 square kilometers of far northern Queensland, from the rainforest to the bushlands. They range in size from an eight-student elementary school with one teacher-principal to a high school with over 600 students. The quality and quantity of information available at each of the sites varies. We found two that were of particular interest. The Mareeba State Primary School site (P-7) has information about Aboriginal and Torres Strait Islander people and culture authored by the students. You might also want to pay a visit to the students and staff of the Herberton State School (8-10) to learn about their town and school. They also have a detailed section on Australiana written by the students that covers such topics as Aboriginal traditional medicine, weapons, and hunting; crocodiles and other animals; the Kakadu National Park; the Great Barrier Reef; Australia in World War I and II; Lionel Rose (an Australian boxer); Christmas in Australia; and the Australian desert.

SCHOOLS—CANADA

See Chapter 2—Canada—Lake Academy—Fortune, Newfoundland *and* Leo Ussak School—Canadian Arctic.

SCHOOLS—GERMANY

Patch American High School—Stuttgart, Germany

http://192.253.114.31

Patch American High School is operated under the auspices of the Department of Defense for children of military personnel stationed in Stuttgart, Germany. Your students will enjoy viewing the variety of work produced by these very busy students. They give you their perspective on the visit of Astronaut Susan Still, who talked about prelaunch training, in-orbit activities, and her life. Share the students' other activities, including the Army Junior ROTC and Internet class. Or, take a multimedia tour of the Patch Barracks, the headquarters for the United Station European Council. The students will then take you on a tour of Stuttgart (including the Mercedes-Benz and Porsche Museums), Augsburg, and the Carnival in Basel. If you still have the energy, you will want to read about the Arab-Israeli conflict and visit the students' detailed exhibits on the Berlin Wall, World War II, and stereoscopes.

See also Chapter 1—World War II; Chapter 2—Germany—On-line Tour #3; *and* Chapter 10—Photojournalism.

SCHOOLS—ISRAEL

See Chapter 3—Natural Wonders—Deserts.

SCHOOLS—JAPAN

American School in Japan Elementary

http://www.asij.ac.jp/content.html

The 475 students that attend the nearly century-old American School in Japan (ASIJ) come from 43 countries. Meet the students and join in their activities, such as martial arts. They will also tell you how they feel about living in Japan and share local traditions, including Koto music, tea ceremonies, fashions, shodo (calligraphy), and flower arranging.

For other information contained in this site, see Chapter 5—Concerts and Musical Adventures.

Nagatsuka Elementary School

http://www.csi.ad.jp/school/project/nagatuka/index.html

A major focus of the students at the Nagatsuka Elementary School is the study of peace. Students have developed the *1,000 Cranes* project in which peace messages are exchanged on a worldwide basis. Perhaps the nuclear attack on Hiroshima has such a large impact on the students because their "schoolmaster" lived through the experience. Your students will be interested in his firsthand account of the A-bomb incident as related through his story, "The Summer When I Was a First Grader in Elementary School—August 6, 1945."

SCHOOLS—NEW ZEALAND—SCIENCE FAIR

http://www.actrix.gen.nz/biz/ecnz/proj.html

Take your students to the virtual New Zealand Science Fair. Finalists from the junior and senior high schools will show you their projects. Each year, approximately 40 New Zealand students are chosen from approximately 40,000 entrants. Projects include the Mite of the Mite, Arachnid's Phobia, Fixed Speed Cameras, War of the Roses, and Tea Treatment for Smelly Socks.

SCHOOLS—UNITED STATES—ALASKA

North Slope Alaska School District

http://www.nsbsd.k12.ak.us/villages/akp/nuna1.htm

The Anaktuvuk Pass Nunamiut project was designed by students, teachers, photographers, federal agencies, and the local curator. Experience the past and current ways of the inland Eskimos or the Nunamiut from Anaktuvuk Pass. Students will take you on a tour of the local cultural museum and share their essays and photographs.

SCHOOLS—UNITED STATES—ILLINOIS

Highland Middle School—Libertyville

http://www.elk-grove.k12.il.us/schoolweb/highland

Meet the teachers and join in the activities of middle grade students of the Highland School. Of special interest is the project on tessellation math in which students use the tessellations of M. C. Escher in order to realize the importance of math in the art world. Students create their own Escher-type tessellations through the modification of a polygon to create nonpolygon tessellating shapes.

See also Chapter 6—Escher, M. C.

SCHOOLS—UNITED STATES—MASSACHUSETTS

Nantucket Elementary School

http://www.nantucket.net/schools/cps

The students at Nantucket Elementary School and the Cyrus Pierce Middle School will take you on an historical tour of the island, during which you will learn such interesting facts as why all of the streets are made of cobblestone. You might also be interested in the simulated Republican Convention by the eighth-grade class.

SCHOOLS—UNITED STATES—NEW YORK

Cayuga Heights Elementary School—Ithaca

http://k12.cnidr.org/gsh/schools/ny/che.html

The students at Cayuga Heights have been working hard on their energy project. Your students can participate in the project while learning about past and present uses of electricity and gas. They can read a story from an 1852 utility booklet and try to find ten energy uses (if you can't find them, the students will give you the answers), use math to try to figure out an 1859 gas bill, and learn about heating, lighting, and cooking through the ages. If you have time, stop by and meet the staff and the students.

Dr. Charles R. Drew Science Magnet School—Buffalo, New York

http://drew.buffalo.k12.ny.us

Meet the students and teachers of this grade 4-8 school. See their current Internet projects and let them take you on a tour of the Buffalo Museum of Science and the Buffalo Zoological Gardens.

See also Chapter 3—Zoos, Farms, and Animals—Buffalo Zoological Gardens.

SCHOOLS—UNITED STATES—OHIO

Olmsted Middle School—Olmsted Falls, Ohio

http://www.leeca.esu.k12.oh.us/ofcs/ms/ofms.html

Enter the home page of the Olmsted Middle School for a personal welcome from the principal. Join the eighth-grade students in building a mousetrap-powered vehicle using the principles of power, forces, and machines. Send in your plans. Winners will become part of the MTVP Hall of Fame. Feel free to browse the current hall of fame. You can also participate in other activities with the students, such as an Internet Hunt.

SCHOOLS—UNITED STATES—OREGON

Buckman Elementary Magnet Arts School—Portland, Oregon

http://buckman.pps.k12.or.us/buckman.html

Visit the students and staff of this magnet school in Portland. You are welcome to enter each of the classrooms and see what these grade 1-5 students have been learning. The first-grade class, for example, has designed a space alphabet book in conjunction with their space science unit. You can view the book and even hear the students read. They are very prolific authors, as evidenced by the other on-site books you will be able to read. They have also been busy studying about bubbles, penguins, bees, and Hovercraft. The students will explain and illustrate the concept of floating on a cushion of air. You might prefer to take a video tour of the room and, if you have time, play a few games on site with the students.

Vose Elementary School—Beaverton, Oregon

http://www.beavton.k12.or.us/vose/home.html

The Vose Elementary School holds the distinction of being the first school in the Pacific northwest built in a circular shape. The K-5 students have developed an on-line "kidopedia," an interactive encyclopedia with articles contributed by students throughout the world. You can browse the work by topic or by letter. See the site to see how you can contribute articles.

SCHOOLS—UNITED STATES—TEXAS

Hightower High School—Missouri City

http://chico.rice.edu/armadillo/ftbend/btrleson.html

Read about, see, and join in projects with students and teachers of the Hightower High School. Projects have included units on Texas rivers, the monarch butterfly, and weather. The school also hosts a worldwide show and tell.

SCHOOLS—UNITED STATES—VIRGINIA

Christianburg High School—Christianburg

http://www.bev.net/education/schools/chs/index.html

Visit the staff and students of Christianburg High. Accompany them to their field trip to Anderson and Associates where they learn about Geographical Information Systems. Then return to school and visit the art department and *Doodleville*, a gallery of "artwork" completed by students after their assignments are done.

SCHOOLS—UNITED STATES—WASHINGTON

Alderwood Elementary School—Bellingham

http://wwwald.bham.wednet.edu/museum/museum1.htm

Alderwood Elementary School in Bellingham, Washington, has constructed a web site that pays homage not only to Ellis Island, but also to United States immigrants. *Our Immigration Wing* chronicles stories that students from Cambodia, Greece, Russia and the Ukraine, Mexico, and Vietnam have written about their families' culture and immigration to the United States. These reports include photographs. *The Ellis Island Wing* contains photographs of and information about Ellis Island, including a fifth-grade student's report. The site also contains information and artifacts from a student who is a member of the Lummi Nation, including pictures and text about baby boards, God eyes, and paddles and dolls.

Bellingham High School—Bellingham

http://wwwbhs1.bham.wednet.edu

The students of Bellingham High School realize that the beginning of career planning should take place during the high school years. In this effort, they have established the *Career Pathways* project, which profiles various careers and the steps necessary to achieve them. Visit the school, see the students' work, and meet the staff who have inspired it.

Fairhaven Middle School—Bellingham

http://wwwfms.bham.wednet.edu/lobby.htm

Explore the school's virtual museum to learn about turn-of-the-century life in Fairhaven, Washington, at one time the salmon capital of the world.

Kulshan Middle School—Bellingham

http://wwwkms.bham.wednet.edu/lobby.htm

The students and teachers of this school have established a Pacific Rim Museum of Culture, where a variety of artifacts and documents are displayed. The museum deals with the cultural diversity of the Pacific Rim.

SCHOOLS—UNITED STATES—WYOMING

Monroe Middle School—Green River

http://monhome.sw2.k12.wy.us/west/west.html

The seventh and eighth graders of Monroe Middle School have established the *Web Witch of the West's Fun Page,* where you can learn all about Green River and other areas of Wyoming. The students will show you photographs of and tell you about Wyoming's wildlife (from avocets to snowshoe hares). Perhaps you would prefer to tour the area's national parks. The students will be happy to take you on tours of Yellowstone National Park, Devil's Tower National Monument, Grand Teton National Park, and the Flaming Gorge National Recreation area. Or, if you prefer to go back in time, they'll tell you all about the Oregon Trail. The eighth graders traveled the trail on foot and will share their photographs, excerpts from their fictional journals and actual nineteenth-century pioneer journals, and some of the trail's history. If you prefer to stay indoors, they'll entertain you with their movie, book, and television reviews, sports, and hobbies.

SCIENCE

Astronomy Lessons

See Chapter 4—On-Line Astronomy Course.

Earth Science Lessons

See Chapter 2—Antarctica—On-line Tour #2.

CHAPTER 12

Meet Famous People

Tired of waiting for someone famous to visit your school? Then take a trip to meet them, unhampered by agents, press secretaries, managers, or long lines. Historical figures, authors, poets—they're all waiting to teach and entertain your students.

AMIS, MARTIN

http://www.albion.edu/fac/engl/diedrick/amispge.htm

Students can get to know Martin Amis through published interviews, biographical materials, excerpts from his works, and photographs. Among other things, Amis talks about how having a famous father (Kingsley Amis) and attending 14 schools by the time he was 19 years of age affected his views of narrative theory. There are excerpts from Amis's novels and samples of his reviews, including his review of Hillary Rodham Clinton's *It Takes a Village*. There are also reviews of Amis's own works.

ANGELOU, MAYA

See Chapter 5—Lectures and Speeches—Michigan State Writers Lecture Series.

ARNETT, BISHOP

See Chapter 1—African American History—Library of Congress—American Memory.

ARNOLD, BENEDICT

See Chapter 1—American Revolution—Williamsburg, Virginia.

ASIMOV, ISAAC

See Chapter 5—Lectures and Speeches—Michigan State Writers Lecture Series.

ATWOOD, MARGARET

See Chapter 5—Lectures and Speeches—Michigan State Writers Lecture Series.

AUDUBON, JAMES

See Chapter 3—Parks and Sanctuaries—Corkscrew Swamp Sanctuary.

AUSTEN, JANE

See Chapter 10—Austen, Jane.

BANKS, ERNIE

See Chapter 1—African American History—Negro Leagues Baseball Online Archive.

BERNIER, ROSAMOND

See Chapter 5—Lectures and Speeches—Michigan State Writers Lecture Series.

BLAKE, WILLIAM

See also Chapter 10—Blake, William.

http://www.aa.net/~urizen/blake.html

You know that a William Blake site is going to have great graphics. Richard Record, a computer programmer and Blake enthusiast, wants to show your students the complete text and color plates of *Songs of Innocence* and *The Marriage of Heaven and Hell*. In addition, there are a dozen of Blake's paintings, including *Satan Inflicting Boils Upon Job*. There is also extensive biographical material and articles addressing how his poetry and art were inextricably entwined.

BOLEYN, ANNE

See Chapter 2—United Kingdom—Tower of London.

BONESTELL, CHESLEY

See Chapter 6—Chesley Bonestell Art Gallery.

BONNEY, THERESE

See Chapter 1—World War II—Female Journalists, Photographers, and Broadcasters of World War II.

BOORSTIN, DANIEL J.

See Chapter 5—Lectures and Speeches—Michigan State Writers Lecture Series.

BORGES, JORGE LUIS

http://www.rpg.net/quail/libyrinth/borges.html

Borges, the linguistic illusionist, would love this site, which pays homage to the man, his thoughts, and works. In addition to the biographical material one would expect, there are images of the Argentinean author that have been "tweaked" to create surreal effects and even postcards. There is a generous selection of Borges quotations, taken from both his fiction and nonfiction. (One of our favorites is his comment on a translation: "The original does not do justice to the translation.") There are selections from his works, including several that have never been translated from Spanish. In addition, there are instructions for joining a free Borges Internet mailing list.

BRADLEY, OMAR

See Chapter 1—World War II—Patch American High School Exhibit.

BROWN, JOHN

See Chapter 1—African American History—Library of Congress—American Memory.

BUBLEY, ESTHER

See Chapter 1—World War II—Female Journalists, Photographers, and Broadcasters of World War II.

BURNS, ROBERT

http://www.robertburns.org

Meet the famous Scottish poet and learn all about his life, songs, and poems; the people he knew; and the places he lived and visited. There are also detailed instructions for hosting a Burns's supper on the traditional date of January 25. (If you're going to serve haggis, don't invite us.) To help you communicate with Burns, the site provides a glossary of Scottish terms.

BURROUGHS, JOHN

http://www1.mhv.net/~omi/jb.htm

Burroughs (1837-1921) was known as America's most beloved nature writer. Students can view copies of letters written throughout his lifetime, photographs, and copies of some of his works. There are also biographic and bibliographic materials and several Burroughs' quotations, filed by subject.

BUSH, GEORGE, AND BARBARA BUSH

http://csdl.tamu.edu/bushlib

Some of the important events that occurred during George Bush's presidential term included the end of the Cold War, the beginning of democracy in eastern Europe, the passage of the Americans with Disabilities Act into law, and the reunification of Germany. Read about these events and meet George and Barbara Bush through exhibits at the George Bush Presidential Library and Museum. Follow Bush's career through his service at the United Nations, the Central Intelligence Agency, Congress, and as the president. Materials include his major speeches (organized chronologically), an extensive collection of photographs (most of them of Bush's public life, rather than private), biographies of Bush and his wife Barbara, and information on Barbara Bush's Foundation for Family Literacy. This site was still under construction at press time, so new materials are constantly being added.

CAMPANELLA, ROY

See Chapter 1—African American History—Negro Leagues Baseball Online Archive.

CAMPBELL, BEN NIGHTHORSE

See Chapter 6—Native American Art—Powersource Gallery.

CARROLL, LEWIS

See Chapter 6—Web Museum.

CARTER, JIMMY, AND ROSALYNN CARTER

http://sunsite.unc.edu/lia/president/carter.html

This site is under construction. However, detailed biographical material on Jimmy and Rosalynn Carter are currently available, along with photographs. Of particular interest is the exhibit on the Camp David Accords, which outlines the diplomatic history leading to the Camp David meetings and discusses the physical setting of and preparations necessary for hosting the meetings, the day-to-day negotiations (using Carter's memoirs), and the impact of the meetings on modern history.

CEZANNE, PAUL

See Chapter 6—Monet, Claude.

CLASSICAL COMPOSERS

http://spight.physics.unlv.edu/picgalr2.html

The *Picture Gallery of Classical Composers* contains dozens of portraits, each accompanied by cursory biographical information. Composers can be selected either alphabetically or by their nationality; we searched by nationality and discovered that the gallery exhibits at least a half-dozen Mexican classical composers, who are usually overlooked by most other classical music sites.

CLEMENS, SAMUEL

See Twain, Mark, *below*.

CLEVELAND, GROVER

See Chapter 5—Lectures and Speeches—Michigan State University Vincent Voice Library.

CLINTON, WILLIAM JEFFERSON, AND HILLARY RODHAM CLINTON

See Chapter 2—United States—Washington, D.C.—White House *and* Chapter 5—Lectures and Speeches—Michigan State University Vincent Voice Library.

COCHISE

See Chapter 6—Native American Art—Powersource Gallery.

COLLINS, WILKIE

http://www.ozemail.com.au/~drgrigg/wilkie.html

Only on the Internet would you travel all the way to Australia to visit a minor Victorian writer. Wilkie Collins, a contemporary and friend of Charles Dickens, wrote a series of stories and novels fitting into the genre then known as "sensation fiction." Today, the works would be classified as a combination of detective and horror fiction. Obtain information about Collins and some of his best-known works (*The Woman in White* and *The Moonstone*) and see illustrations from his books.

CONROY, PAT

See Chapter 5—Lectures and Speeches—Michigan State Writers Lecture Series.

COOLIDGE, CALVIN

See Chapter 1—World War I.

COX, JAMES

See Chapter 1—World War I.

CRAIG, MARY

See Chapter 1—World War II—Female Journalists, Photographers, and Broadcasters of World War II.

CRANE, STEPHEN

http://www.en.utexas.edu/~mmaynard/Crane/crane.html

Professor Michele Maynard of the University of Texas English Department has constructed this web page as a "collaboratory [*sic*] project" with her class. Hear sound clips of people reading *The Open Boat*, *The Blue Hotel*, and *The Red Badge of Courage*. Students can also read Crane's biography and see photographs. You are not likely to find out anything about Crane here that you didn't already know, but the sound clips and the photographs are worth the trip.

DA VINCI, LEONARDO

http://www.leonet.it/comuni/vinci

Pay a visit to the Leonardo da Vinci Museum and show your students what a Renaissance genius could do. The east wing contains his oil paintings, including, of course, *The Mona Lisa* and *The Last Supper*. The west wing contains reproductions of Leonardo's engineering and futuristic designs, with accompanying texts. Your students will certainly be interested in how a man born centuries before the Wright Brothers designed a helicopter. The north wing has additional da Vinci drawings and sketches, and the south wing has a text on Leonardo's life and the times in which he lived.

DAHL, ROALD

http://www.wolfenet.com/~jmeaney/roald_dahl.html

Roald Dahl has received renewed attention with the release of Disney's *James and the Giant Peach*. See cover illustrations and reviews and actual Dahl works, with an emphasis on children's literature. Obtain a biography and photographs.

DALI, SALVADORE

http://www.empower.net/dali/dalimain.html

Haven't you always wondered what went on in the mind of Salvadore Dali? This exhibit presents biographical materials and critical commentary on the various phases of his career, as well as describing major influences in his life. There is also an exhibit of his works.

D'AMBOISE, JACQUES

See Chapter 5—Lectures and Speeches—Michigan State Writers Lecture Series.

DEPRIEST, JAMES

See Chapter 5—Concerts and Musical Adventures—African-American Classical Composer Archives.

DOCTOROW, E. L.

See Chapter 5—Lectures and Speeches—Michigan State Writers Lecture Series.

DOUGLASS, FREDERICK

See Chapter 1—African American History—Library of Congress—American Memory.

EARHART, AMELIA

See Chapter 5—Lectures and Speeches—Michigan State University Vincent Voice Library.

EASTMAN, GEORGE

http://www.eastman.org

This site was created by students in the advanced certification program in Interactive Media Development at the Rochester Institute of Technology—a way of paying back the man who was practically Rochester's *raison d'etre*. The students examine the life of George Eastman (1854-1932) through photographs and biographical material.

For other information contained in this site, see Chapter 6—Photography and Photojournalism—George Eastman House.

ECO, UMBERTO

http://www.rpg.net/quail/libyrinth/eco.html

Meet the Italian author of fiction, essays, academic texts, and children's books. Eco, a professor of semiotics at the University of Bologna is known for his playful use of language, symbols, and puzzles and his narrative inventions. Students can view biographical materials, summaries of reviews of his works, quotes, and photographs of the author.

EISENHOWER, DWIGHT DAVID

http://sunsite.unc.edu/lia/president/eisenhower.html

Some of the most memorable events in history transpired during Eisenhower's term of office. It was during this time that the Department of Housing, Education, and Welfare was created; the Korean War ended; the Geneva Accords were signed; the historical Brown v. Board of Education of Topeka decision was made; federal funding for the construction of interstate highways was established; the 1957 Civil Rights Act was passed; both Sputnik and Explorer I were launched, and Alaska and Hawaii became states. Learn about and see some of these highlights of Eisenhower's term of office and read about his life and civilian, military, and political careers. There is also information on his family.

ESCHER, M. C.

See Chapter 6—Escher, M. C.

ESTES, SIMON

See Chapter 5—Concerts and Musical Adventures—African-American Classical Composer Archives.

FAULKNER, WILLIAM

http://www.mcsr.olemiss.edu/~egjbp/faulkner/faulkner.html

Mississippi honors its native son at this site with commentaries, plot synopses, a biography, Faulkner's family tree, a bibliography and filmography, trivia, quotations, and a glossary. There is also information on Oxford, Mississippi, Faulkner's home town.

http://www4.ncsu.edu/unity/users/s/sbcain/faulkner.html

This site is especially appealing for those who have sound capabilities on their computers because it contains audios of Faulkner reading his Nobel Prize acceptance speech and excerpts from *The Old Man* and *As I Lay Dying*. The acceptance speech, with its stirring conclusion that man will not only endure but prevail, is always a favorite with high school students. Those without audio capabilities should connect to the previous Faulkner listing.

FAWKES, GUY

See Chapter 2—United Kingdom—Tower of London.

FLANNER, JANET

See Chapter 1—World War II—Female Journalists, Photographers, and Broadcasters of World War II.

FLEETWOOD, CHRISTIAN

See Chapter 1—African American History—Library of Congress—American Memory.

FLEMING, IAN

http://www.mcs.net/~klast/www/fleming.html

Students can learn all about John F. Kennedy's favorite author—the creator of the James Bond novels. The site contains photographs, biographical material, articles, and interviews. Students can also view his personal library and the site of his grave and learn the truth about Fleming's rumored connections to the CIA. Skip the section "The Secret of Goldeneye"—it's an advertisement.

FORD, GERALD

http://www.lbjlib.utexas.edu/ford/homepage.htm

Although most of this site is still under construction, there are approximately 100 of the most requested photographs from the Gerald Ford Library on display, as well as transcripts of some of Ford's speeches. The events covered range from his childhood to the current time and include such historic moments as the Nixon pardon and Ford's inaugural. The site for the Ford Presidential Library is http://http2.sils.umich.edu/FordLibrary.

FRANKLIN, BENJAMIN

See Chapter 1—American Revolution—Williamsburg, Virginia *and* Chapter 9—Science—Museums—General—Franklin Institute Science Museum *and* Invention Dimension.

FRISSELL, TONI

See Chapter 1—World War II—Female Journalists, Photographers, and Broadcasters.

FULLER, BUCKMINSTER

http://www.pbs.org/wnet/bucky.cgi

Meet the captain of "Spaceship Earth." This colorful 1960s architect, designer, engineer, poet, philosopher, and author, one of the earliest people involved in the ecology movement, is best known for the geodesic dome. Materials at this site are from a television show funded by the National Endowment for the Humanities and the National Endowment for the Arts with American Express corporate sponsorship. There are interviews, pictures of Fuller domes, textual material, and photographs.

GABLE, CLARK

See Chapter 9—Science—Museums—Aviation and Aerospace—United State Air Force Museum.

GALILEO

See Chapter 9—Science—Museums—History—Institute and History of Science Museum of Florence, Italy *and* Renaissance Science.

GERARD, JAMES WATSON

See Chapter 1—World War I.

GERONIMO

See Chapter 6—Native American Art—Powersource Gallery.

GILBERT AND SULLIVAN

See Chapter 5—Operas and Operettas.

GOMPERS, SAMUEL

See Chapter 1—World War I.

GORE, ALBERT, AND TIPPER GORE

See Chapter 2—United States—Washington, D.C.—White House.

HAN, BETTY

See Chapter 6—Photography and Photojournalism—George Eastman House.

HARDING, WARREN G.

See Chapter 1—World War I.

HAWTHORNE, NATHANIEL

http://www.tiac.net/users/eldred/nh/hawthorne.html

Although your students may not find this quite as appealing as Demi Moore in *The Scarlet Letter*, they will be able to gain a more accurate depiction of Hawthorne and his works. This site contains illustrated Hawthorne novels, biographical materials, and audio readings of some of his works.

HEANEY, SEAMUS

http://sunsite.unc.edu/dykki/poetry/heaney

Heaney is deemed by some to be the most important Irish poet since William Butler Yeats. Your students will be able to make their own decision about this as they read about, see, and hear this 1995 Nobel Prize winner's poetry, biography, and speeches.

HELLER, JOSEPH

See Chapter 5—Lectures and Speeches—Michigan State Writers Lecture Series.

HEMINGWAY, ERNEST

http://ww.ee.mcgill.ca/~nverever/hem/pindex.html

Students can pay a visit to *The Papa Page* and see Hemingway photographs, obtain biographical material and a bibliography, read quotations, and see his collection of paintings. The material covers Hemingway's roles as a hunter, soldier, and writer, and follows his life through Oak Park, Illinois, to Italy in World War I, to Paris, to Spain during its civil war, to Cuba, to Europe in World War II, to his final days in Utah.

HENRY, PATRICK

See Chapter 1—American Revolution—Williamsburg, Virginia.

HOOVER, HERBERT

http://sunsite.unc.edu/lia/president/hoover.html

Herbert Hoover lived through some of the most exciting and harrowing times in history, such as the "roaring twenties" and the "war on a thousand fronts." The Herbert Hoover Library opened on the 88th birthday of this 31st president, known throughout the world as the "Great Humanitarian." The facility has over 7 million pages of document holdings, a generous sample of which are available via this site. There are detailed biographical materials covering Hoover's life and the events of the eras during which he lived. Additional material is constantly being added. Site proprietors promise a section with educational modules, which may be available by the time *Virtual Field Trips* is in your hands.

HUGO, VICTOR

See Chapter 5—Theater—Les Miserables.

JEFFERSON, THOMAS

See also Chapter 1—American Revolution—Williamsburg, Virginia.

http://www.monticello.org

How would you like to spend an entire day with Thomas Jefferson? You'll have to begin early, as Jefferson has had a lifelong habit of rising out of bed the minute it is light enough to see the hands on his clock. Absorb the views and historical artifacts in the various rooms at Monticello while Jefferson participates in his usual activities: reading, writing, eating, visiting. . . . You can accompany him on every one of these activities.

Wait until you see his inventions, such as the "clothes turning machine," a kind of precursor to the moving racks in dry cleaner shops. At the end of the day, Jefferson dies (on July 4th) and his epitaph, per his request, mentions the three things he considered to be his greatest accomplishments: writing the Declaration of Independence, composing the Virginia Statutes (concerning religious freedom), and founding the University of Virginia.

To view the university site, see Chapter 2—United States—Virginia—University of Virginia.

JOBS, STEVE

See Chapter 9—Science—Museums—General—Invention Dimension.

JOYCE, JAMES

http://www.2street.com/joyce

Your students can hear Joyce reading passages from his book *Finnegan's Wake* and hear the actual song that gave Joyce the title. There are articles on Joyce, maps, a biography with a timeline, photographs of Joyce and the people and places that influenced him, complete texts of Joyce's major novels, an electronic journal devoted to Joycean scholarship, the landmark Supreme Court decision ruling that *Ulysses* was not obscene, information on joining a Joyce electronic mailing list, and a list of actual, noncyberspace James Joyce reading groups who meet around the United States.

KENNEDY, JOHN FITZGERALD

http://webcorp.com/civilrights/jfkinaug.htm

Hear speeches from JFK's inaugural ceremony. We suggest that you supervise the use of this site because there are direct links to materials that you may consider inappropriate.

KENNEDY, JOSEPH

See Chapter 1—World War II—National Archives and Records Administration Exhibit Hall.

KING HENRY VIII

See Chapter 2—United Kingdom—Tower of London.

KING, MARTIN LUTHER JR.

http://www.seattletimes.com/mlk

The *Seattle Times* newspaper, a leader in the movement to have Martin Luther King Day declared an official national holiday, invites you on a tour of King's life. You can see photographs and read texts pertaining to key events in the struggle for civil rights, read a dialogue about King between students in Alabama and Washington, take a quiz (which is scored on site), and hear sound clips from King's speeches. There is also a study guide consisting of open-ended questions designed to encourage classroom discussion about key civil rights issues. King's famous Washington civil rights speech can be found at http://www.webcorp.com/civilrights/mlk.htm. (We suggest you monitor the use of this site because it has direct links to material that you may consider inappropriate.)

http://www-leland.stanford.edu/group/King

The Dr. Martin Luther King, Jr., Center for Non-Violent Social Change invites you to tour their facility, where they have an extensive collection of texts by and about Dr. King.

LANGE, DOROTHEA

See Chapter 1—World War II—Female Journalists, Photographers, and Broadcasters of World War II.

LEROUX, GASTON

See Chapter 5—Theater—Phantom of the Opera.

LINCOLN, ABRAHAM

See Chapter 8—The Lincoln Museum *and* National Archives and Records Administration.

LOUIS, JOE

See Chapter 9—Science—Museums—Aviation and Aerospace—United States Air Force Museum.

LUCE, CLARE BOOTH

See Chapter 1—World War II—Female Journalists, Photographers, and Broadcasters of World War II.

MAILER, NORMAN

See Chapter 5—Lectures and Speeches—Michigan State Writers Lecture Series.

MALCOLM X

http://www.unix-ag.uni-kl.de/~moritz/malcolm

Elke Moritz, a 27-year-old computer science student in Germany who is interested in African American studies, has constructed this memorial to Malcolm X. In addition to numerous photographs, the exhibit includes Ossie Davis's famous eulogy, transcripts of Malcolm X interviews, a long excerpt from one of his well-known speeches, and a long series of quotes by and about Malcolm X.

MARQUEZ, GABRIEL JOSE GARCIA

http://www.rpg.net/quail/libyrinth/garcia.marquez.frame.html

This Columbian-born writer and resident of Mexico City is considered to be one of the pioneers of magical realism. Students can learn about this Nobel Prize–winning author through biographical material, by reading about events that shaped his life (including a detailed history of Columbia), and through a gallery of photographs, paintings, and book covers.

MAYS, WILLIE

See Chapter 1—African American History—Negro Leagues Baseball Online Archive.

MCCARTHY, JOSEPH

http://www.webcorp.com/mccarthy

Beginning with the timeless quote from Santayana—"Those who forget about the past are condemned to repeat it"—this site takes your students back to the 1950s era of McCarthyism, where they can hear a some of Senator Joseph McCarthy's speeches. Hopefully, they will gain new appreciation for the principles of democracy. In addition to McCarthy's speeches and photographs, students can hear the speech by the Council for the Army that effectively ended the McCarthy era—Welch's famous, "At long last, sir, have you no shame?" From here, you can link to a collection of "speeches" made by current politicians, which have been randomized: meaningless phrases and clichés have been strung together to produce familiar sounding speeches that say nothing.

MCMILLAN, TERRY

See Chapter 5—Lectures and Speeches—Michigan State Writers Lecture Series.

MILLER, ARTHUR

See Chapter 5—Lectures and Speeches—Michigan State Writers Lecture Series.

MILLER, KELLY

See Chapter 1—African American History—Library of Congress.

MONET, CLAUDE

See Chapter 6—Monet, Claude.

MONROE, JAMES

http://pulex.med.virginia.edu/highland/default.htm

Students can visit with James Monroe at his Ash Lawn-Highland estate, where he resided from 1799-1826. The tour takes you through the grounds of the estate and through various rooms, showing such articles as a watch belonging to Mrs. Monroe and their bed—complete with trundle board. There is a brief Monroe biography and explanation of Ash Lawn-Highland as a working plantation (with no mention of slaves). The history of Ash Lawn-Highland is interesting, explaining as much about the young United States as about the property. The estate was adjacent to Jefferson's property, and when Monroe went overseas as an ambassador, Jefferson arranged to have the orchards planted. In Monroe's later years, his wife became ill, his finances became strained, and he was forced to sell Ash Lawn-Highland.

MUIR, JOHN

http://www.sierraclub.org/john_muir_exhibit

You may wish to prepare for this field trip to the Sierra Club's John Muir exhibit by downloading the K-12 teacher's guide. The field trip includes a John Muir photo gallery (not nature photos, but photos, drawings, and woodcuts of Muir himself), Muir's writings, geography cards that explain the connection between Muir and various parts of the world, and an extensive bibliography. The *News and Upcoming Events* section includes the latest copy of the *Muir Newsletter*, as well as reviews of films and books about Muir or the Sierra Club.

NIGHTINGALE, FLORENCE

See Chapter 5—Lectures and Speeches—Michigan State University Vincent Voice Library.

NIXON, RICHARD M.

See also Chapter 8—National Archives and Records Administration.

http://www.webcorp.com/video/nixon

There may not be a United States president, including Lincoln, who made more famous speeches than Richard Nixon, though they are remembered for different reasons. Now your students can hear some of Nixon's most memorable speeches, such as the famous "Checkers" speech, his "last press conference," and comments made during Watergate. This site takes a cynical view of Nixon, so you may wish to balance it with other materials.

OATES, JOYCE CAROL

See Chapter 5—Lectures and Speeches—Michigan State Writers Lecture Series.

PAIGE, SATCHEL

See Chapter 1—African American History—Negro Leagues Baseball Online Archive.

PATTERSON, MARVIN BRECKENRIDGE

See Chapter 1—World War II—Female Journalists, Photographers, and Broadcasters of World War II.

PERSHING, JOHN

See Chapter 1—World War I.

POCAHONTAS

See Chapter 6—Native American Art—Powersource Gallery.

POE, EDGAR ALLAN

http://www.cs.umu.se/~dpcnn/eapoe/ea_poe.html

Try to convince your students that it is Edgar Allan Poe, rather than R. L. Stine, who deserves credit for the detective and horror genres. You may have more luck if you take them to this site, which contains biographical materials, copies of his stories and poems, and direct links to his home and the Edgar Allan Poe museum. Certainly Poe led a more interesting life than Stine; the biographical information includes sketches of family members, and it puts many of his works into an historical and biographical context. The information is so complete that there is even a discussion of the latest theory that Poe died from rabies. There is also a Poe chatroom, where students from around the world (mostly college students) can exchange questions, information, and thoughts about Poe. One word of caution: This site comes from Umea University in Sweden, and there are many misspellings.

PRESIDENTS, UNITED STATES

http://sunsite.unc.edu/lia/president

Did you know that the "Buck Stops Here"—the saying that Harry Truman was so famous for—was originally from a federal reformatory in Oklahoma? The sign on his desk could be reversed to show the expression "I'm from Missouri," depending on his mood and who was in his office. These and other facts can be found in various presidential libraries and biographies accessible from this site. As of the date of publication, much of the material was still under construction. Those sites that were available as of the date of publication are discussed in this chapter under the names of the applicable president.

PRICE, LEONTYNE

See Chapter 5—Concerts and Musical Adventures—African-American Classical Composer Archives.

PUCCHI, ANCHISE

See Chapter 6—Electronic Art.

PULITZER PRIZE WINNERS

http://www.pulitzer.org

Your students can meet past and present winners of the renowned Pulitzer Prize.

For other information contained in this site, see Chapter 5—Pulitzer Prize Board.

RALEIGH, SIR WALTER

See Chapter 2—United Kingdom—Tower of London.

REAGAN, RONALD

See Chapter 9—Science—Museums—Aviation and Aerospace—United States Air Force Museum.

RICHARD II AND RICHARD III

See Chapter 2—United Kingdom—Tower of London.

RIVERA, DIEGO

See Chapter 6—Diego Rivera Museum.

ROBINSON, JACKIE

See Chapter 1—African American History—Negro Leagues Baseball Online Archive.

ROOSEVELT, FRANKLIN DELANO, AND ELEANOR ROOSEVELT

See also Chapter 1—World War I.

http://www.academic.marist.edu/fdr/fdrintro.htm

Presidential libraries exist largely because of Roosevelt. Prior to his presidency, presidential papers were the property of the individual and their distribution or disposal was left to chance. FDR was instrumental in the passage of the act that made presidential materials the property of the public. Visit the Franklin Delano Roosevelt Library in Hyde Park, New York, to learn about Roosevelt and his family and see exhibits from his life—from his christening dress (1884) to his grave. There is a searchable database of FDR speeches and papers, as well as a link to the FDR Museum, which features exhibits on the people and main events instrumental to his presidency. Teachers interested in the New Deal may wish to check out the New Deal Database, which includes actual archived and real-time simulated press conferences provided by the New Deal Network, an organization devoted to examining the programs and policies of the New Deal.

ROSS, BETSY

http://www.libertynet.org/iha/betsy/index.html

The story of Betsy Ross is one of triumph over adversity. Meet Ms. Ross and learn how she overcame exile from the Quakers and the loss of three husbands and two infant daughters. You will be able to read the story of how she sewed the first American flag, take a tour of her house, and even learn how to cut a five-pointed star in one strip—she taught

George Washington the same skill. There is also information on the flag, including flag etiquette, trivia, and a photo gallery. Do you know who was the only person in history honored for cutting the American flag into pieces? Visit Betsy Ross and she'll tell you all about it.

ROSSETTI, DANTE GABRIEL

See Chapter 6—The Rossetti Archive.

RUTH, BABE

See Chapter 5—Lectures and Speeches—Michigan State University Vincent Voice Library.

SADAT, ANWAR

See Chapter 5—Lectures and Speeches—Michigan State University Vincent Voice Library.

SITTING BULL

See Chapter 6—Native American Art—Powersource Gallery.

STEWART, JIMMY

See Chapter 9—Science—Museums—Aviation and Aerospace—United States Air Force Museum.

STILL, JUDITH ANNE

See Chapter 5—Concerts and Musical Adventures—African-American Classical Composer Archives.

TERRELL, MARY CHURCH

See Chapter 1—African American History—Library of Congress—American Memory.

TESLA, NIKOLA

http://www.neuronet.pitt.edu/~bogdan/tesla

Bogdan Kosanovic, a Ph.D. in electrical engineering, has put together this homage to the man who held over 500 patents on such inventions as fluorescent lights, AC power transmission, rotating magnetic fields, the induction motor, and the radio. Visit Tesla at Niagara Falls, New York, and the Chicago World's Fair of 1893, as he displays his latest inventions. He will share his views, occasionally acerbic, on everything from Edison to science. You will also be able to read what others have to say about him. The collection of Tesla anecdotes includes his boyhood experiment with wings: He stood on a roof, hyperventilated until he felt light-headed, and then jumped. There is also a Tesla photo album.

THOREAU, HENRY DAVID

http://www.envirolink.org/elib/enviroethics/thoreauindex.html

Thoreau, whose insistence on integrity still inspires students today, is one of those writers who always seems relevant. Now your students can access his biography and his most important writings, as well as some of his travel journals.

TRUMAN, HARRY S., AND BESS TRUMAN

http://sunsite.unc.edu/lia/president/truman.html

Long before the concept of the sound bite, Harry S. Truman's colorful sayings, such as "If you can't stand the heat get out of the kitchen," captured worldwide attention. Best known for his controversial Hiroshima decision, the 33rd president of the United States had a long and colorful life (1884-1972). The 18,000-square-foot Harry S. Truman museum captures the personality of Truman through photographs, original documents, and biographical materials. There is also information on his wife and his daughter Margaret—best known for her mystery novels. At the time of publication, education modules were under construction.

TRUMAN, MARGARET

See Chapter 12—Truman, Harry S., and Bess Truman.

TWAIN, MARK

http://interact.courant.com/special/twain/index.htm

What better way to experience Mark Twain than by visiting this site, hosted by the *Hartford Courant*, the newspaper in the town where Twain lived much of his adult life? Through photographs, contemporary newspaper accounts from the *Courant's* archives, and Twain's own words, Twain, as he himself might put it, comes as close to being alive as he's ever likely to get. The site is divided into *The Man*, which includes a timeline of Twain's life with accompanying photos, a photo album, various newspaper clippings on Twain, and biographies of his wife, daughters, and brother; *The Writer*, which includes bibliographies of Twain's works and books written about him, a collection of anecdotes culled from *The Courant's* files, a 10-question quiz on Twain, and articles about Twain written by Dan Rather, Kurt Vonnegut, and Lewis Lapham; *His World*, which includes biographies and reminiscences of people who were close to Twain, including the family maid; and *Twain Today,* which takes you on a tour of Twain's Hartford home. The entire site is packed with photographs.

http://www.iijnet.or.jp/robagoya/mt/mtpage.htm

One can only imagine what Mark Twain would say about traveling to Japan to learn about him, but this is exactly what you can do via the Internet. This site, from the Robagoya-juku English School in Tokyo, is a pictorial homage to Twain. If you are looking for photographs of places from Twain's Missouri childhood, you will want to take this quick trip to Japan.

WARHOL, ANDY

See Chapter 6—Andy Warhol Museum.

WASHINGTON, BOOKER T.

See Chapter 1—African American History—Library of Congress—American Memory.

WASHINGTON, GEORGE

http://www.history.org/people/washhdr.htm

"His bones and joints are large, as are his hands and feet, all the muscles of his face are under perfect control, though flexible and expressive of deep feeling when moved by emotion. In conversation he looks you full in the face, is deliberate, deferential and engaging." Your students can spend some time with this great man through the efforts of the Colonial Williamsburg Foundation. Follow George Washington from his birth to his final day, when he succumbs to "inflammatory quinsy."

For information on Colonial Williamsburg, see Chapter 1—American Revolution—Williamsburg, Virginia.

WATSON, DOC

http://sunsite.unc.edu/doug/DocWat/DocWat.html

Doc Watson was writing and performing bluegrass music long before such modern performers as Alison Krause were born. Two University of North Carolina faculty members have put together this exhibit with biographic materials and sound recordings. Fans of the legendary North Carolina musician will appreciate the complete on-site discography and concert schedule.

WELLS, IDA B.

See Chapter 1—African American History—Library of Congress—American Memory.

WHITE, CLARENCE

See Chapter 6—Photography and Photojournalism—George Eastman House.

WILLIAM THE CONQUEROR

See Chapter 2—United Kingdom—Tower of London.

WILLIAMS, TENNESSEE

http://www.susqu.edu/ac_depts/arts_sci/english/lharris/CLASS/WILLIAMS/table.htm

Meet and see the famous playwright and follow his colorful life from 1911 to 1983.

For other information contained in this site, see Chapter 5—Theater—The Glass Menagerie.

WOLFE, THOMAS

http://www.cms.uncwil.edu/~connelly/wolfe.html

Travel to Chapel Hill, North Carolina, Thomas Wolfe country, to experience the life of the famous author (1900-1938). Your tour begins with a Wolfe quotation of the week (new quotes each Friday afternoon), and then it's on to the Thomas Wolfe Memorial and the photograph gallery. The exhibits include biographical materials, a bibliography, and reviews of Wolfe's works.

WOZNIAK, STEVE

See Chapter 9—Science—Museums—General—Invention Dimension.

WRIGHT, FRANK LLOYD

http://www.swcp.com/FLW/tourthenat.html

Let the Frank Lloyd Wright Conservancy introduce you to the famous architect and some of his notable works. You will be able to tour the country and view such Wright-designed buildings as the Guggenheim Museum in New York and houses in Wisconsin and Illinois.

http://flw.badgernet.com:2080

Visit this site for additional materials on Frank Lloyd Wright, including photographs and a gallery with still images and videos. You will even be able to hear a speech by the famous architect.

WYTH, GEORGE

See Chapter 1—American Revolution—Williamsburg, Virginia.

CHAPTER 13

Field Trips to Primary Grade Sites

Are you tired of taking your students to the local apple farm? Perhaps they may be more interested in traveling to Australia or playing inside of an ant hill. After all, even the youngest students deserve to see the rest of the world sometimes!

ANIMAL SOUNDS

http://www.georgetown.edu/cball/animals/animals.html

Cathy Ball, at Georgetown University's Department of Linguistics, wants to show your students how different languages can turn a simple cow's moo into the Tower of Babel. For example, although a bee may sound the same in Spain and Japan, the Spanish sound is translated as *zzz*, while the Japanese sound is translated as *bun, bun*. There are several dozen animals speaking through audio files and printed phonetics in well over a dozen languages. You can search by animal or by language. By choosing, for example, Greek, Hebrew, or Korean, you will get a list of the animals (in that language) followed by the phonetic sound each makes and a link to the sound file.

ANT HILL

http://sec.dgsys.com/antfarm.html

Take your students on a visit to a local ant hill where the denizens will provide them with both knowledge and fun. The ants will share word searches, jokes, and stories. In return, they ask you to help them find their way out of their mazelike hill. There are also ant facts (e.g., what is the only place in the world an ant cannot live?) and even famous quotes about ants by such notables as Ben Franklin, who said, "None preaches better than the ant, and she says nothing."

AUNT ANNIE'S CRAFTS PAGE

See Chapter 11—Arts and Crafts Classes—Aunt Annie's Crafts Page.

AUSTRALIA

http://www.ozemail.com.au/~wprimary

Students can hear the laugh of a kookabura, color a rainbow lorikeet, make a climbing koala, fly a sugar glider kite, and make a hopping kangaroo.

BEAR CUB DEN

See Chapter 3—Zoos, Farms, and Animals—Cub Den.

CALIFORNIA LIVING MUSEUM

See Chapter 3—Zoos, Farms, and Animals—California Living Museum.

CARLOS' COLORING BOOK

http://www.ravenna.com/coloring

This is an on-line coloring book that features pages with leprechauns, Easter eggs, and other primary grade-appropriate pictures. Unlike other sites on the Web, this allows the kids to color on screen, rather than printing the picture and then coloring.

CHILDREN'S STORYBOOKS ONLINE

http://www.magickeys.com/books/index.html

This site contains a frequently changing collection of easy-to-read illustrated books. However, you may wish to choose your books carefully and ahead of time because this is primarily an on-line subsidy publisher. Books that are presented have not gone through a rigorous editorial selection process; rather, authors pay to have them published on line.

D DOG'S HOUSE

http://www.aha-kids.com/ddog.htm

This site is produced by Al Hyslop, who also has produced *Captain Kangaroo*, *Sesame Street,* and *3-2-1 Contact*. Children can interact with D Dog and his best friend Mike in a series of games and primary level crafts, such as coloring, mazes, or building a planter out of a juice box. D Dog keeps a scrapbook on line, and he wants children to draw a picture and send it to him. Both kids and teachers will like D Dog's Celebrity Sandwich Shop. When we last checked, Robin Leach revealed his secret for making a peanut butter and jelly sandwich so that no jelly seeps through the bread and all over your hands. Other topics are D Dog's Bulletin Board, Cowboy Jim Bob's Read to Me Page, and D Dog's Dog Show. You may wish to avoid D Dog's Toy Store, which is a commercial for toys and other products.

DISNEY INTERACTIVE STORYBOOK

http://www.disney.com/DisneyBooks/Readastory/_index.html

A new Disney story is added to this site each month. Click on the book to select such illustrated stories as *Aladdin*, *The Hunchback of Notre Dame*, *The Lion King*, *Oliver and Company*, *Pocahontas,* and *Toy Story*. All other paths on this site are commercials for Disney products.

DODOLAND

http://www.swifty.com/azatlan

This site, sponsored by numerous nonprofit organizations, is dedicated to helping small children develop a respect and appreciation for our planet, the environment, and each other. The concept of Dodoland as a fun place where children learn respect for all living things began as a book about 20 years ago in Los Angeles, became a play in New York City, and has since spawned workshops in creative writing, art, music, dance, and drama. The site is updated every two months. A typical "issue" of Dodoland begins on giant Flower Island, where kids have a choice of writing, learning environmentally oriented games, or, in one wonderfully imaginative segment, clicking on a photo of a rainbow and finding themselves right near the gaping jaws of a hippo. They can then click inside the hippo's yawning mouth and end up just outside the ancient city of Machu Picchu, covered with clouds. In another segment, kids send an e-mail message of their wish for the Earth, and they can read what other kids have submitted. (One child wrote, "Please help the Earth. It's crying out to you like the eagle child.")

GRANDAD'S ANIMAL ALPHABET BOOK

http://www.maui.com/~twright/animals2/htmgran.htm

Kids can learn the alphabet in English or Spanish with *Grandad's Animal Alphabet Book.* Grandad has an animal and poem for every letter (the Xuprocar is an animal from another planet). After exploring the various sections on the alphabet, animal classifications, and animal facts, your students can take the quiz at the end, which will automatically be scored.

KENDRA'S COLORING BOOK

http://www.gcg.com/misc/colorbook

This site contains an interactive coloring book that allows users to color pictures from a specified list. They can color their own picture or start from where a previous user left off. There are 14 colors that can be mixed in various combinations.

MR. ROGERS' NEIGHBORHOOD

http://www.pbs.org/rogers

It's a beautiful day in the neighborhood, so why not take your kids to visit Mr. Rogers? He will share the words to his favorite and most familiar songs. Be sure to visit the *Children's Corner,* where kids can choose one of Mr. Rogers' characters and scenes to color and explore. For example, in a scene from Make-Believe Land, kids can not only color but also answer the question, "How many different ways are characters saying, 'I love you'?" At Mr. Rogers' Parents' Page, you can find many simple activities and articles on such topics as helping kids to deal with anger or change. For example, to spur a discussion about change, the site suggests you have your child examine a piece of bread before and after toasting it.

MR. STIX'S ELECTRONIC TREEHOUSE

http://www.interlog.com/~brucem

Mr. Stix is an electronic drummer and kids' musician. He is more than happy to let young children play in his *Fun Centre*. (Everything outside the Fun Centre is information about Mr. Stix, who is available for concerts and parties.) There are lyrics to popular sing-a-longs, such as *Wheels on the Bus,* riddles and knock-knock jokes, and pictures to color. If you're looking for party ideas, Mr. Stix has about a dozen suggestions for games. Mr. Stix will even let children inside his music room, where they can play his electronic "domino" drums on the computer. (He tells you how to download the free software to enable this.) There are also several interactive activities. Kids can read a story in which they choose the direction the story will take and supply sound effects. Or, they can write lyrics to their own nonsense song, using Mr. Stix's fill-in-the-blanks format.

NORTH POLE

http://www.the-north-pole.com

Is there a better place than the North Pole for children to celebrate the holiday season? If you don't want to travel that far, Rudolph and the elves will accept e-mail. If you decide to take the trip, be prepared—the elves and Rudolph seem to have some problems getting along. Follow the path *Good Help Is Hard to Find* and listen to the elves complain about constant interruptions and all of the attention that Rudolph gets. Meanwhile Rudolph is willing to share his recipes for elf logs (his revenge on the elves) and algae newtons. If you would rather not get involved in their quarrels, choose the path *Christmas in Our Village* and attend plays or listen to carols and stories. Santa will read *The Night Before Christmas* or sit back while your class reads and he provides sound effects. Your students may also help the villagers decorate their digital Christmas trees, choosing from a variety of trees and ornaments.

OUTER SPACE

See Chapter 4—National Aeronautics and Space Administration (NASA)—NASA—StarChild.

POOH'S PAGE

http://worldkids.net/pooh/welcome.html

There are over 20 places to visit in Pooh's 100 Acre Woods, including Roo's Sandy Place, Tigger's Bouncing Spot, the Piknik Spot, and Where the Woozie Wasn't. Pooh and his friends are great hosts and will keep visitors busy in each of the places they visit. For example, learn how to make pawprint cookies, honey treats, and a very warm drink for a very blustery day at Pooh's recipe page. There are also downloadable coloring book pages and a section of children's poems and artwork. Among numerous other awards, the site was selected as a Safe Kids Site.

PROFESSOR BUBBLES' BUBBLESPHERE

http://bubbles.org

This award-winning site has information provided by Professor Bubbles, who has appeared on television shows and concerts worldwide. Pay him a visit and he will show you his bubble inventions and how to make your own bubble tools, share a recipe for the ultimate bubble solution, teach you the history of bubble blowing, and more.

RAINY DAY RESOURCE PAGE

http://www.cp.duluth.mn.us/~sarah

If you want to keep your students occupied during indoor recess, have them pay a visit to this page where they will find recipes for playdough (both edible and inedible), bubbles, silly putty, oobleck, etc., and instructions for making paper airplanes, pine cone bird feeders, and more.

WEBTIME STORIES WITH WEBSTER

http://www.webtimestories.com

This site is for "little webcrawlers." The path *Children* has on-line books in easy-to-read illustrated formats. We suggest you avoid the paths *Gifts* and *Webster's Clubhouse*, where the commercials reside.

Index